Introduction to Theft, All Risks

# Introduction to Theft, All Risks and Money Policies

## D Cutter

### Series editor: R M Walmsley

Croner Publications Ltd
Croner House
London Road
Kingston upon Thames
Surrey KT2 6SR
Tel: 081-547 3333

Published by
Croner Publications Ltd,
Croner House,
London Road,
Kingston upon Thames,
Surrey KT2 6SR
Telephone 081-547 3333

While every care has been taken
in the writing and editing of this book,
readers should be aware that only Acts of Parliament
and Statutory Instruments have the force of law,
and that only the courts can authoritatively
interpret the law.

British Library Cataloguing in Publication Data
Cutter, D.
Introduction to theft, all risks and money policies.
(Insurance in practice).
1. Great Britain. Insurance
I. Title II. Series
368.941

ISBN 1-85452-067-9

A *Books Books Books* title

Typeset by Concept, Crayford, Kent.
Printed by Whitstable Litho Ltd, Whitstable, Kent.

# Contents

# Series preface

The day to day practice of insurance involves making decisions in relation to the interpretation of contract documents.

It is a practical job concerned with real problems for real people, and the books in this series are primarily intended to give essential basic information to insurance and professional students which will enable them to understand the principles involved in their work.

In addition, people insured in a private capacity and officials of insured companies need to understand those principles underlying the contracts into which they have entered. Thus this series should also be of value to them, both in the negotiation stage of arranging insurance cover and later when questions arise in relation to a claim.

The various authors are engaged in the claims field and thus the texts are based on practical experience.

R M Walmsley
Birmingham
July 1989

# Introduction

This book is written, as others in the series, to assist students of insurance and people in business generally to understand the way in which the policy conditions apply in practice, and interpret information brought together from various sources.

The importance of basic principles and the fact that these principles apply to insurance generally can be seen from the fact that some legal cases quoted relate to a variety of "insurance situations", not only arising from theft, etc.

As so often in discussion about insurance, there is misunderstanding on the part of the public at large about the nature of the contractual relationship and the contract conditions.

In the classes of insurance referred to in this book, for example, the relationship of "theft" as defined in the Theft Act 1968 (qv) and the cover actually given by the policy is not always recognised.

The question of reasonable care in the context of these covers has been considered by the courts in recent years and it would appear that they are beginning to take a more liberal view of this concept. This means, of course, that insurers must also understand the terms of the contracts into which they have entered.

Whilst Mel Walmsley, as series editor, suggested changes in the original draft, the material and opinions presented remain my responsibility.

I acknowledge the permission of the Association of British Insurers to reproduce the Statement of Insurance Practice. I also offer my thanks to the Sun Alliance Insurance Group for permission to reproduce the policy documents and proposal forms. These policy documents are particularly valuable in demonstrating one of the many wordings used to provide, not only the basic insurance protection considered by this book, but also some wider options available.

D Cutter
July 1990

# CHAPTER 1

# The contract

## Introduction

Whenever a purchase is made, so far as English law is concerned, a contract has been entered into by two or more people. Making a purchase — buying a tangible object — is a process easily envisaged. Insurance, like other services, is an intangible thing. This is recognised by the fact that although we speak of buying an insurance policy, insurance is not in fact considered "goods" for the purposes of the Sale of Goods Act 1979. Indeed, because of the special features of insurance, as we shall see later, the Unfair Contract Terms Act 1977 and other consumer regulations do not apply either.

Insurance students have been taught that the customer buys a promise to do something in the future. This is too simplistic. Nothing is in fact bought. What happens is that a contract is made between two or more parties: the insurance company or underwriter and the persons named in the policy. The latter may be individuals, limited companies or other legal "persons".

The steps leading up to the formation of the contract are frequently managed by an agent or insurance broker but no attempt will be made here to encompass the law relating to agency.

All simple contracts arising in English law require certain essential elements. If one of these elements is missing, there will not be a binding and enforceable contract. A contract for insurance not only needs these basic elements, but also some additional ones.

The essential elements for all contracts are:

(a) an unqualified offer;
(b) unqualified acceptance;
(c) valuable consideration;
(d) legality;

(e)  absence of fraud;

(f)  capacity of the parties to contract.

## Offer and acceptance

Offer and acceptance should be considered together. What constitutes an offer is frequently misunderstood. A price tag on a washing machine in a shop window is not an offer to sell: it is known as an "invitation to treat" — that is, an invitation to the public at large to make an offer to buy. So, newspaper advertisements for car insurance, even those giving examples of premiums, are not offers capable of legal acceptance unless the advertisement makes it clear that that is the advertiser's intention.

Compare the cases of *Pharmaceutical Society of Great Britain v Boots Cash Chemists* (1953) and the best remembered case in English contract law *Carlill v Carbolic Smoke Ball Company* (1893), both of which considered the elements of offer and acceptance.

In the former case the shop, Boots, operated on the now common "supermarket" system of goods displayed on shelves so that customers selected their choice and paid at a cash desk. It was held that the contract was made at the cash desk when the cashier accepted the customer's offer to buy.

In the latter case, the defendant advised the use of its smoke ball as a means of preventing influenza and in the advertisement for it offered £100 to any person who, having used it according to the directions, nevertheless contracted influenza. Mrs Carlill used the smoke ball in accordance with the instructions but still caught the disease and her husband pursued an action on her behalf against the Smoke Ball Company. One of the defendant's arguments in its defence was that Mrs Carlill had not communicated her acceptance of the offer made in the advertisement. The Court of Appeal held, however, that where an offer is made in return for doing an act, the doing of the act is sufficient acceptance.

Reaching the stage of offer and acceptance in an insurance contract is frequently a complex matter. Each party to the potential contract will wish to find out precisely with whom the contract is being made and what its terms are to be.

Generally, the basic wording of the insurance policy will not be negotiable. The insurers have policies which they will not usually vary. Negotiations, therefore, will relate only to premiums and any special terms and arrangements which are required.

The potential insurer may advertise, or send out brochures and provide proposal forms, but just as in a purchase from a shopkeeper, it is generally accepted that the first offer comes from the prospective policyholder or "insured".

Temporary insurance cover may be requested and given at short notice, especially if an insurer is approached by a reliable broker acting on behalf of a prospective insured, but this cover will be confirmed only upon receipt, consideration and acceptance of a completed and satisfactory proposal form. The completed proposal form is the potential policyholder's offer to enter into a contract of insurance.

The appropriate premium is frequently known at that stage as it can be calculated from the insurer's normal rates. If the premium is tendered with the proposal form, acceptance takes place when the insurer acknowledges to the proposer that the insurance contract is in force.

In some cases, the insurer becomes the offerer. For example, by requesting a previously uncalculated premium after receiving the proposal form. The payment of the premium or the agreement to pay the premium by the proposer is then the acceptance.

## Valuable consideration

Valuable consideration is one of the essential elements required to make a valid contract.

The premium is, of course, the valuable consideration provided by the policyholder. The promise to pay claims in the future is the valuable consideration provided by the insurer.

It is worth looking at the reference to valuable consideration in the judgement in *Carlill v Carbolic Smoke Ball Company*.

## Utmost good faith

The proposal form enables the insurer to obtain relevant information about the proposer and the property to be the subject of the insurance contract. It will shortly be seen why the proposer and insurer have a duty to reveal other relevant information not requested by the proposal form.

Insurance companies employ their own surveyors who may visit premises and assess buildings and their contents on behalf of the insurer. When this is done, then facts which the surveyor ought reasonably to have obtained need not be disclosed by the proposer.

Most people have heard the legal warning *caveat emptor* — let the buyer beware. English law recognised more than 200 years ago that such a principle had no place in negotiations for a contract of insurance. It was, and still is, essential that each party has full knowledge of the intentions of the other. Hence the insurance contract is clearly identified by the words of the policy and policy schedule, and prior to the contract coming into force and during its currency each party is governed by the principle of "utmost good faith".

This principle of utmost good faith in insurance contracts was eventually embodied in statute — The Marine Insurance Act 1906 s. 17. The rule was clearly stated, however, in 1766 by Lord Mansfield during his judgement in the case of *Carter v Boehm*.

> Insurance is a contract upon speculation. The special facts, upon which the contingent chance is to be computed, lie more commonly in the knowledge of the insured only: the Underwriter trusts to his representation, and proceeds upon confidence that he does not keep back any circumstance in his knowledge, to mislead the Underwriter into a belief that the circumstance does not exist and induce him to estimate the risk as if it did not exist. The keeping back of such a circumstance is a fraud and therefore the policy is void. Although the suppression should happen through mistake, without any fraudulent intention; yet still the Underwriter is deceived and the policy is void; because the risk run is really different from the risk understood and intended to be run at the time of the agreement. . . . Good faith forbids either party by concealing what he privately knows, to draw the other into a bargain, from his ignorance of that fact and believing the contrary.

### Binding on both parties

This principle binds both the proposer and insurer. The Marine Insurance Act 1906 makes this clear even if Lord Mansfield's flowery phrases do not: "if utmost good faith is not observed by either party the contract may be avoided by the other party".

The fact that the insurer is also bound was recently confirmed in a Court of Appeal case, eventually reported as *Banque Financière v Westgate Insurance Company* (1989).

This complicated case, the original hearing of which took three months to complete, involved fraud on a number of banks as well as an insurance company. The Court of Appeal decision confirmed not only that good faith bound both parties but also that the remedy for breach of the duty of utmost good faith will not normally (in the absence of fraud) enable the aggrieved party to obtain the remedy of damages.

There are, however, few instances where the insurer has failed to provide information known to it to the detriment of the policyholder. If there have been such instances, it is likely that the insurer would have sought a compromise in the interests of good consumer relations. Most reported cases on the principle of good faith have arisen because the insurer has maintained that the proposer has not demonstrated good faith in the contract negotiations.

The following words arose in the judgement of *Brownlie v Campbell* (1880):

> in policies of insurance... there is an understanding that the contract is Uberrima Fides, (that is utmost good faith), that, if you know any circumstance at all that may influence the underwriter's opinion as to the risk he is incurring, and consequently as to whether he will take it, what premium he will charge, if he does take it, you will state what you know ... and the concealment of a material circumstance known to you, whether you thought it material or not, avoids the policy.

## Material fact

It will be seen, then, that the proposer has a duty to reveal "material circumstances", or as it is described today "material facts". Typical proposal forms used by insurers are designed to elicit most facts considered by the insurer to be material, but if there is other material information which *may* influence an underwriter's opinion, that information must be made available. (See Appendix for a specimen proposal form which shows the type of information which should be disclosed.)

How can a proposer know what is a material fact, that is, how can the non expert know what the expert considers essential? The Marine Insurance Act 1906 s. 18 (2) states:

> every circumstance is material which could influence the judgement of a prudent insurer in fixing the premium or determining whether he will take the risk.

What then is a prudent insurer? Unfortunately there is no definitive answer! The proposer must bear in mind words of Lord Salvesten in the Privy Council case of *Mutual Life Assurance Company of New York v Ontario Metal Products Company Limited* (1925).

It is a question of fact in each case whether [the information] would, on a fair consideration of the evidence, have influenced a reasonable insurer to decline the risk or to have stipulated a higher premium.

There can be only one answer for the proposer: answer all the proposal form questions fully and if there is other unrequested information, reveal that also.

For example, in the case of *Bufe v Turner* (1815) it was held material that there had been a fire in premises adjacent to the building for which insurance had been arranged. Indeed, the fire in question occurred on the day that the insured in this case told his agent to arrange insurance. A fire in the adjacent premises broke out again two days later and spread to the then insured building. It was held that the insurers were entitled to know of the original fire as this was a material fact. As this material fact had been withheld from them they were entitled to avoid the policy.

It has been accepted that the following are not considered material facts and need not, therefore, be disclosed:

(a)  Facts which the insurer knows, or may reasonably be expected to know. For example, matters of public knowledge or the law of the land.
(b)  Facts which the insurer can obtain by normal enquiries.
(c)  Facts about which the insurers waive information.
(d)  Facts which tend to lessen the risk.

It has already been seen that the result of failure to disclose material facts is that the aggrieved party may avoid the policy. That is, the contract is avoidable at the option of the prejudiced party.

It does not matter that non-disclosure results from fraud, carelessness or ignorance; the result is the same. The insurer may refuse to honour what would have been its part of the bargain had the full facts been available to it. Premium is only returnable if the non-disclosure is innocent and no part of the risk ever attached; that is, the insurer was never at risk of having to make a payment for a claim.

If the proposer, innocently or otherwise, gives incorrect information rather than not providing information at all, the effect of this "misrepresentation", if it is material, is the same as non-disclosure.

It should be emphasised that the duty of disclosure does not arise from a term of the contract itself. It arises outside the contract and applies to all contracts of a similar nature, for example partnerships. Consider *March*

*Cabaret Club and Casino Limited v London Assurance* (1975). Here, the reasoning of Scrutton L J in *Rozanes v Bowen* was emphasised. Namely, that the disparity in negotiating strength between the proposer who knew everything and the insurer who knew little of the risk must mean that the duty arose outside the contract (see Appendix).

## Declaration

The proposal form has already been mentioned. It is necessary now to look at the declaration against which the proposer places his or her signature:

> I declare that the foregoing statements and particulars are true and complete and that this proposal shall form the basis of the contract with (the Company) . . .

The significance of this declaration will be appreciated bearing in mind the doctrine of utmost good faith already considered. This part of the declaration, relating to a proposal for theft insurance and also, so far as it does, to the business, premises and property to be insured, ensures that if any of the information is incorrect the policy may be avoided by the insurer.

In the case of *Mackay v London General Insurance Company Limited* (1935), Mr Mackay completed his proposal form and answered in the negative a question asking whether any insurer had refused, cancelled or declined to accept or renew similar insurance. In fact, when he was a minor another insurance company had imposed a, then, substantial excess. He also answered in the negative a question asking whether he had been convicted or had his driving licence endorsed. In fact he had been fined for having a vehicle without efficient brakes.

The current insurer declined policy liability on the grounds that Mr Mackay had inaccurately and incorrectly answered questions on the proposal form.

In giving judgement, Mr Justice Swift expressed the view that he was certain that even had Mr Mackay answered the questions accurately and correctly, he would still have been granted insurance on this occasion and went on to say:

> I am quite satisfied that both of these answers were quite immaterial; . . .
> I am extremely sorry for the plaintiff in this case. I think he has been very badly treated — shockingly badly treated — but I cannot help the position.
> Sorry as I am for him there is nothing that I can do to help him. The law is quite plain.

... the plaintiff has contracted that the proposal and declaration shall be the basis of the contract between him and the said company and in the proposal, he has made two answers which I cannot say were accurate.

Much as I sympathise with him, I am bound to say that the company were within their rights when they repudiated their liability under this policy; and I must dismiss this action with costs.

It should be pointed out at this stage that insurers now agree to bind themselves voluntarily to a code of practice designed to relieve policyholders *in their private capacity only* from the consequences of innocent non-disclosure and misrepresentation, and any failure to comply with warranties in certain circumstances.

The code of practice is the Association of British Insurers Statement of General Insurance Practice. The document is reproduced in full in the Appendix, but the relevant features are that it has been voluntarily agreed that the declaration on the proposal form should be restricted to completion according to the proposer's knowledge and belief, and that an insurer will not refuse to indemnify on the grounds of non-disclosure or misrepresentation if the circumstances of the loss are unconnected with the breach (unless fraud is involved).

# CHAPTER 2

# *Security*

## Introduction

From the theft insurer's point of view, the more difficult it is to gain entry to a building, the safer will be the contents from loss or damage by thieves, and the insurer will not be prepared to insure property of any value within a building unless satisfied that the building is protected to a degree appropriate to the contents.

Buildings differ in the extent to which they are or can be made secure. The degree of security must, from an insurance point of view, reflect the nature and value of the property inside. The more valuable, desirable and mobile the property within, the greater will be the security demanded by the insurer before insurance cover will be granted.

A policyholder owning a modest business with predictable stock and trade machinery may only be required to confirm that certain protections are in force and will be maintained. For example, doors should be fitted with five lever mortice deadlocks and windows should have lockable catches.

## Surveyor's report

The possibility of a burglary surveyor attending the premises has already been mentioned. The surveyor's report will advise the insurer's underwriter what protections are at present in force and what ought to be installed by way of replacement or in addition to those measures already in existence in order to provide adequate protection for the contents in question. It may be that the existing protections are totally inadequate, in which case insurance cover will not be provided until they are improved.

Frequently, however, insurance cover is provided following an agreement that the policyholder will ensure that the required protections are in force in a specified time. Insurance cover will cease after that time if the agreement is not complied with.

The insurers may require the fitting of an alarm system before cover is confirmed. Frequently the make and specification of the alarm will be agreed in advance and in addition a maintenance contract may be required.

## Warranty

The insurance underwriter considers the nature and protection of the premises to be vital when considering the premium required.

In order to ensure that the protections are maintained and used, the insurer may attach to the policy a warranty (more commonly known today as a "condition precedent to liability under the policy"). In English contract law, a warranty is a term of a contract which is not of fundamental importance, that is, it does not go to the root of the contract. Where a party is in breach of a *warranty* the other party is entitled to damages but not to rescind the contract. A *condition* in contract law is something vital to the agreement, a breach of which enables the aggrieved party to avoid the contract and sue for damages as well.

However, in insurance contracts the situation is different. An insurance warranty has the weight of a contract condition and *vice versa*! So, a breach of a warranty by the policyholder in the insurance contract will enable the insurer to repudiate liability under the policy.

This reversal of the effects of conditions and warranties in insurance contracts is confirmed in the Marine Insurance Act 1906 s. 33 (3):

> A warranty . . . is a condition which must be exactly complied with whether it is material to the risk or not. If it be not so complied with . . . the insurer is discharged from liability.

In the theft policy a warranty frequently included in the premises section of the schedule is:

> It is warranted that the building of which the premises form a part is otherwise normally inhabited as a private residence by the insured or by an employee of the insured charged with the care of the premises.

Frequently, of course, this warranty is inappropriate, in which case it can be deleted. It serves, however, to demonstrate that the insurer still uses the word warranty in its insurance sense.

Additional warranties required by the insurer will be added by way of an endorsement affixed to the policy by glue, staple or binding. An endorsement is an addition to or variation of the policy, usually (though not essentially) in writing. When affixed to the policy the endorsement forms part of it and has equal weight with all other words and clauses.

To make the importance clear, each clause or endorsement which is an insurance warranty normally begins with the words "it is warranted that" or more commonly today "it is a condition precedent to any liability under this policy that".

Endorsements attached to theft policies relating to the nature of the protections to the premises when unattended vary in wording depending upon the insurer's requirements. If the protections are considered satisfactory, such an endorsement may read as follows:

> It is a condition precedent to any liability under this policy that the premises shall not be left without a responsible adult therein unless all the security devices and protections existing at the date of this endorsement including any mentioned hereunder are in full and effective operation . . . subject to the terms and conditions contained in the policy.

To emphasise the point the use of the words "it is a condition precedent to liability under the policy" makes it clear that the insurer intends the endorsement, as an insurance warranty, to go to the root of the contract and any breach may enable it to avoid making a payment in the event of a claim.

Consider the case of *Victor Melik and Company Limited v Norwich Union and Kemp* (1980). The plaintiff insured a warehouse against theft of contents via the agency of the second defendant. The alarm condition on the policy read as follows:

> It is a condition precedent to liability that:
>
> (a) The burglar alarm installed at the premises is kept in efficient working order.
> (b) The maintenance contract company is immediately advised of any defect.
> (c) The burglar alarm is kept in full operation at all times when the premises are unattended.

Following a loss by theft, the claim for which was settled under the policy, the insurer required additional work to be carried out to the premises and the alarm, and this was completed. Shortly afterwards a fault developed on the line system which connected the alarm to a control centre (which would of course advise the keyholder and the police). The premises were inspected and it was found that the telephones were not working. The alarm was set to an audible warning only; the maintenance contractor and the GPO were advised and the police were asked to maintain extra patrols. The policyholder was advised by the broker that insurance cover still operated. Shortly after this a further theft occurred and it was subsequently found that thieves had cut the telephone lines in an area which was the responsibility of the GPO.

The insurer repudiated the claim for breach of policy conditions, ie it considered that the alarm had not been kept in efficient order. (There was also an argument about indemnity by the broker which is not relevant to the present discussion.)

It was held that the condition did not require the alarm to be in efficient working order. The condition required it to be "kept" in order and the use of the word "kept" implied with it that there could not be a breach of the condition unless the policyholder was aware of the reason for the alarm not working. It was also held that the alarm itself was at all times in efficient working order and what had failed was the GPO line to the control centre. The defendant was not therefore entitled to avoid liability for breach of condition.

The use of more detailed alarm and protection warranties is quite frequent. In the Appendix there is an example of a particularly demanding type which would be appropriate for property at considerable risk of loss unless strict precautions were taken to prevent it.

# CHAPTER 3

# The theft policy and schedule

## Introduction

It has already been seen that the answers to the proposal form questions provide the information which will be entered upon that part of the policy called the schedule. As will be seen later, one of the conditions of the policy makes it clear that the schedule and policy itself are both evidence of the contract. A typical wording is:

> This policy and The Schedule shall be read together as one contract and any word or expression to which a specific meaning has attached in any part of the policy or of The Schedule shall bear such specific meaning whenever it may appear.

It is the policyholder only who identifies for the purposes of the contract the legal identity of the business, its nature, the premises from where the business will operate and which will, of course, contain the property which is to be insured.

The insured is the person to be indemnified under the terms of the contract and to whom any payment will be made.

The principle of indemnity itself will be considered in some detail in due course. Briefly, for now, a person is indemnified when placed in the same position financially after a loss as he or she was prior to it.

The insured must therefore be a legal person, that is an individual, partnership or a corporate entity. In other words, the insured must be a person or organisation capable of entering into legal obligations. It follows then that upon the death of an individual or the liquidation of a company, the insurance contract will cease to exist unless provision has been made for that contingency in the policy wording. In effect, a new contract arises with the transfer of interest to insure the interest of the executors, administrators or liquidator.

As the insured is the legal person who will benefit from claims payments it is essential in law that he or she has a legal relationship with the property being insured. Indeed, it is not the property that is insured but the insured's interest in it. To allow otherwise would be to return to the situation of more than 200 years ago when individuals could arrange "insurance policies" upon the life of the King, or any other person for that matter, hoping to benefit financially from his early death. Such arrangements are not contracts of insurance, but merely a gamble. This unsatisfactory situation led eventually to legislation — The Life Assurance Act 1774 which made such policies unenforceable.

## Insurable interest

The legal relationship required (which must be based upon a financial interest) in property to be insured is given the obvious title of insurable interest. It was defined by Laurence J in the case of *Lucena v Craufurd* (1806):

> To be interested in the preservation of a thing is to be so circumstanced with respect to it as to have benefit from its existence, prejudice from its destruction.

The most common and obvious insurable interest is ownership, but other relationships may also be sufficient, for example:

(a) contractual obligations;
(b) possession — the insured may be liable for loss to the true owner of goods in his or her possession (hoteliers have such a statutory responsibility);
(c) bailment.

### Bailment

Such a legal responsibility most frequently arises by way of bailment. A bailee is someone who has custody of the property of another, the intention being that the property will be returned to the owner. For example, a motor trader will have possession of a vehicle during repair or service, a dry cleaner possession of clothing for cleaning.

The bailee in such circumstances, where payment for work done will be made, is said to be a "bailee for reward". However, a friend who, without payment, looks after a car during the owner's holiday is a "gratuitous bailee".

The law requires the bailee to return the property. If this is not possible, due to loss or damage, a bailee for reward must be able to prove that the loss or damage occurred in spite of all reasonable care for its protection having been taken. In the case of a trader, this must mean that he or she took such care as might be expected from a trader carrying out his or her duties in an efficient manner appropriate to the business and prevailing circumstances. The duty is high and the onus is upon the bailee for reward to prove that reasonable steps were taken.

A gratuitous bailee will also be held responsible for any loss or damage if he or she fails to take reasonable care of the property, but the onus of proof that he or she did not do so rests with the owner who seeks compensation.

Case law authorities are numerous and varied, and merely confirm that each case must be considered on its merits. However, two cases have made it clear that bailment does not always arise when property is left with another, even when payment is made.

In *Hinks v Fleet* (1986), a caravan was stolen from a site. Mr Hinks owned the caravan and paid rent for a site for it at Mr Fleet's caravan park. The Court of Appeal held that the agreement was a licence to park the caravan and bailment had not arisen, therefore Mr Fleet did not owe a duty of care to prevent the theft.

In *Chappell v National Car Parks* (1987), a car was stolen from a car park after a parking fee had been paid. It was held that as possession of the vehicle had not been transferred there was no bailment, only a licence to park.

Insurable interest can also arise from mortgages granted or held, leases granted or held, trusteeship or custom.

The insured need not specify the nature of the insurable interest when completing a proposal form but, if not the legal owner, must be able to show insurable interest when a claim is made for loss or damage. Certainly the insurable interest must exist at the time of the loss, but the law is not in all respects clear whether or not insurable interest must exist at the time insurance is arranged. The Marine Insurance Act 1906 s. 6 allows insurance to be arranged for an interest yet to exist. In his judgement in the case *Williams v Baltic Insurance Association of London Limited* (1924) Roche J suggested that the same situation existed for motor insurance, and it would be reasonable to conclude that it is a general principle.

Certainly a trader can insure a *class* of property, as clearly a shopkeeper, for example, will have sold the stock existing at the time insurance is taken out and replaced it with similar stock, possibly many times over, before a loss occurs.

One thing is absolutely clear, if a proposer states that he or she has insurable interest at the time of arranging the insurance then that must be true. A policy will not be valid if interest is subsequently acquired. See *Tattersall v Drysdale* (1935).

The case of *Castellain v Preston* (1886) confirms that it is the interest and not the property which is insured.

> What is it that is insured in a fire policy? Not the bricks and the material used in building the house but the interest of the insured in the subject matter of insurance.

It should be mentioned here that since a limited company is a separate legal entity from the shareholders it has its own insurable interest so far as the company property is concerned. The shareholders have no insurable interest in such property — see *Macaura v Northern Assurance Company Limited* (1925). A shareholder in a company was owed money by that company. The shareholder attempted to insure timber owned by the company and the timber was lost in a fire. The insurer refused to pay the shareholder on the basis that he had no insurable interest. The House of Lords' decision was for the insurer.

This would not normally cause any problems, but where one person (or a family) owns all the shares in a limited company, he or she does not, even so, have any insurable interest in the property of that company. The "insured" identified for the purposes of any policy should be the legal owner of the property in question or have some other interest that can be clearly identified.

The policy schedule shows an address for the policyholder. This need not be the address where the business is situated. The address here considered is the postal address to which the policy and other correspondence will be sent.

## The business

The proposal form, correspondence, negotiations and possibly a survey will have identified the business of the proposer. The insurer needs to know the precise nature of the business and exactly what processes, if any, are carried out. It is not sufficient to describe the business as a shop. The nature of the goods sold is a material fact. Cigarettes to the value of £10,000 are in more danger of being stolen than groceries of the same value. A wholesale jeweller may deal in a large volume of relatively cheap items or alternatively a few very valuable gems or pieces. The risk of loss and the likely value of any one loss are different in each case and it is the chance of loss and likely cost of each that will influence the underwriter when the insurance terms and premiums are being considered.

Each policyholder should ensure that the business is clearly and completely described in the schedule so that he or she can be satisfied that the underwriter has been given the opportunity to consider all material facts.

This may be emphasised by the schedule section relating to the property. That section begins by making it clear that only property pertaining to the business (the business described in the schedule) will be considered protected by the policy. Therefore, a confectioner who wishes to sell or hire out video tapes should advise the insurers of that fact, and the management of a steel processing plant that wishes to process copper also should do the same, so that in both cases, special arrangements can be made by the insurers having had the opportunity of considering the extra risk involved.

## The property insured

Given that the property does "pertain to the business" what then is the policy concerned with? The following are typical items for which cover is given.

## Stock

A — Stock and materials in trade the property of the insured and goods in trust or on commission for which the insured is responsible.

Stock has the meaning generally understood in the business world — the goods that a business purchases for resale or processing and resale. Materials in trade are those materials used to process stock and finished items when processing has taken place.

The words "Goods in trust or on commission for which the insured is responsible" are used to provide cover for items of a similar nature to stock and materials in trade but which are not owned by the policyholder. "For which the insured is responsible" means legally responsible and thus having sufficient financial relationship as to create an insurable interest. The belief that the policyholder has a *moral* obligation is not enough to create insurable interest and to establish cover under the policy.

## Machinery, etc

B — Machinery, plant, trade and office furniture, fixtures and fittings and all other contents the property of the insured or for which the insured is responsible excluding stock and materials in trade goods in trust or on commission and property more specifically insured.

The first part of this item provides with the words "machinery plant . . . fixtures and fittings" cover for equipment used in the business; office equipment, processing machinery and hand tools, etc. The use of the expression "for which the insured is responsible" again brings in equipment hired in or leased if the hiring agreement makes the policyholder responsible for each item if lost or damaged.

## All other contents

The term All Other Contents includes
a)  documents manuscripts and business books but only for the value of the materials as stationery with the cost of clerical labour expended in writing up and not for the value to the Insured of the information contained therein

b)  computer systems records but only for the value of the materials together with the cost of clerical labour and computer time expended in reproducing such records (excluding any expense in connection with the production of information to be recorded therein) and not for the value to the Insured of the information contained therein

c)  patterns models moulds plans designs but only for the value of the materials together with the cost of labour expended in reinstatement

d)  so far as the same are not otherwise insured directors' employees' customers' and visitors' tools and other personal effects for an amount not exceeding £__ in respect of any one pedal cycle and £__ in respect of the tools and other personal effects of any person

but to exclude
i)    property referred to in the Exclusions

ii)   wines spirits tobacco cigars and cigarettes except such property kept for entertainment purposes for an amount not exceeding £__

There is, of course, other business equipment which does not fall within that described by the words quoted in the previous paragraph. Namely, unused stationery and office equipment, the general paraphernalia of any business. More important perhaps from the policyholder's point of view are the business records, files, plans, accounts and any other documentation, whether in paper or computer form. The use of the words "all other contents" will include everything, but the problem then arises how to value the business records which the policyholder may rightly consider priceless. Without definition, however, the words "all other contents" would extend the cover to everything in the premises.

Because of the difficulties which would arise in the event of a claim, the policy provides the answer. The clause, later in the policy, headed "All other contents", describes how the amount to be paid is to be calculated in the event of a loss involving company records.

The clause provides for payment by the insurer of the cost of materials (paper and computer software) plus the cost of the labour needed to recreate records. The policy wording makes it clear that no attempt will be made to try to calculate the value to the business of the lost records.

This same clause also limits the amount payable in the event of loss of personal effects of employees, and of wines, spirits and tobacco that may be kept on the premises for entertaining purposes.

### Employees' personal effects

So far as the loss of employees' personal effects is concerned, it will be seen that cover is given only if the property is not otherwise insured. Individual household contents policies normally provide cover for the theft of household goods whilst at the householder's place of employment (some household contents policies may require there to be evidence of forceful entry). Such cover does not attach if the personal effects are used for business purposes, so an employee or director who keeps his or her own property at work permanently for use at work could be without insurance cover if that property was stolen. (That is, the household contents policy excludes the property at the business premises because it is used for business purposes, and the employer's policy will not attach because the employer does not have an insurable interest.) The theft policy, then, provides extra cover in this respect for the insurable interest of employees.

Returning to the wording of item B, there are two exclusions which will have been noticed: "Stock as described in Item A and property more specifically insured".

The latter exclusion is to cater for situations where an insured may specifically insure a special piece of equipment. A complex and essential machine may be insured under an engineering policy to provide wider, possibly breakdown, cover. Computers are frequently insured separately to obtain wider "all risks" cover in view of the special place such equipment has within an organisation. That being the case the theft insurers will not wish to duplicate insurance cover.

## Sum insured

The former exclusion, stock, etc, is already specified in item A with its own sum insured and so must be kept separate to avoid duplication and confusion over policy limits. The sum insured, specified by the policyholder for each item, is usually the basis used by the insurer to calculate the premium due. It should be the full value at risk for each item on the schedule, and not the maximum the policyholder considers likely to be lost in any one incident.

### Premium

The premiums calculated for most businesses reflect the probability of partial loss and the rates applied to calculate the premium due assume that the sum insured reflects the true total value at risk. If the sum insured is low the insurer will not have received what is considered by the underwriter to be sufficient premium for the risk, and will not wish to pay the claim in full. The policy wording makes provision for such an eventuality.

### Seasonal adjustments

Some policies designed for special trades make provision for seasonal, temporary, adjustments to the sum insured. The usual theft policy does not. When specifying the sum insured the policyholder should take seasonal variations into account. The obvious seasonal influence is Christmas in retail and some wholesale businesses. Many trades and businesses have a greater turnover during the periods when they are preparing for their heavier Christmas demand. (This is not necessarily the period *immediately* before Christmas of course.) During such periods, stock and materials in trade are likely to be held at higher levels than at other times. The sum insured should be sufficient to take that into account in order to avoid problems should a loss occur at such a time.

It should not be overlooked that various trades are influenced by different seasons, eg the date of Easter influences the holding of stock in the confectionery trade from manufacturer through wholesaler to retailer.

*Average*

In the event of the sum insured not reflecting the true value at risk at the time of a loss, the insurer is protected against the penalty of not receiving an adequate premium for the risk by application of the principle of average. The policy will contain a clause headed "Average" which usually reads as follows:

> Each item of the property is declared to be separately subject to average. That is to say if the property covered thereby, shall at the time of any loss or damage be collectively of greater value than the sum insured thereon, then the insured shall be considered as being his own insurer for the difference and shall bear a rateable share of the loss or damage accordingly.

This is sometimes known as the underinsurance clause for obvious reasons.

"Each item of property" refers to each item on the schedule, so the clause applies to each independently. If one item is underinsured and the other overinsured, the policyholder cannot seek to transfer the overinsurance to the other item in an attempt to avoid the consequences of underinsurance at the time of a loss.

In the event of underinsurance, therefore, the amount which would be paid in settlement of a claim, is in the same proportion that the sum insured bears to the actual value at risk.

The calculation is a simple one:

$$\frac{\text{Sum insured}}{\text{Value at risk}} \quad \times \quad \text{Agreed loss} \quad = \quad \text{Amount payable}$$

Thus, if stock with a replacement value of £5000 was insured for £4000 then in the event of a loss of say £1000 arising from theft as covered by the policy, the insurer would pay:

$$\frac{£4000}{£5000} \quad \times \quad £1000 \quad = \quad £800$$

It can be seen by applying the formula that in the event of all the property insured under an item of the policy being lost by theft, then the full sum insured will be paid no matter what the extent of underinsurance, as the value at risk and agreed loss would be the same amount.

## The premises

The intention of the insurer is to provide insurance cover against loss by theft from the specified premises and not from anywhere else: ". . . any of the property while within the premises".

It is important therefore to clearly identify the premises in question. This is easily done when the premises occupy a single address, for example a shop, a warehouse or an individual factory.

Sometimes, however, the business premises occupy only part of a building, that is, other rooms and areas within a building are not used by the business described in the schedule. For example, a public house or shop with living accommodation would fall into this category. In that event, the business part of the address must be clearly defined and, unless the policy provides otherwise, only losses by theft from that clearly defined area will be considered.

If the business premises are part of a multi-tenanted business structure, for example an office suite in an office block, or a workshop in a tenanted factory then the premises would have to be described in the schedule with enough detail and accuracy to be completely identifiable without ambiguity.

The premises section of the schedule clearly excludes from cover any part of the premises which might, in general conversation, be considered part of the address of the premises but where the risk of loss is greater than from the main building. An example of such an exclusion would be:

Exclusive of any garden, yard or open space and any outbuilding or other building not connected with the main premises unless specially mentioned.

The reason for this, of course, is that gardens, yards and open spaces cannot be effectively protected against entry by potential thieves, and freestanding outbuildings are more vulnerable than the main building. If protection against theft is required for property in outbuildings, the insurer will wish to give the outbuilding in question special consideration depending upon the nature of the contents and the protection available by way of locks, window bars, etc.

## Period of insurance

The schedule also identifies the period of indemnity. This is the period when the policy is in force. Normally 12 months is chosen but may be varied by agreement, usually to a shorter period. The date of commencement will also be agreed by the parties, usually for the convenience of the policy-holder, eg to commence when a previous policy expires. If the policy specifies a date for commencement, then that will be when the policy cover begins, at midnight of the day before.

Fire insurance policies frequently specify a time when the policy will cease. For example "(if the property) be destroyed or damaged by (the peril) at any time before 4 o'clock in the afternoon of the last day of the period of insurance . . .".

When a policy does not specify a time, but merely states that cover will operate from one date to another, it was decided in the case of *South Staffordshire Tramway Company v Sickness and Accident Assurance Association* (1891) that the first date is excluded and the second date included. The policy can, of course, specify that both dates are either included or excluded.

If an insurance policy is issued by the insurer without reference to a date of commencement (an unlikely situation), there is a presumption that the policy is in force whether the premium has been paid or not. See *Kelly v London and Staffordshire Fire Insurance* (1883).

Once in force, the policy will continue to a date specified unless cover ceases because:

(a)   a payment of the full sum insured has been made (in respect of one or more claims) unless the policy specifies that the sum insured may be reinstated after each loss and action has been taken to reinstate it;
(b)   the parties agree to cancel;

(c)  statute operates — for example, a declaration of war may have a
     material effect because of the nationalities of the parties;
(d)  there has been a breach of condition (see later).

If the insurance arrangement has been mutually satisfactory, the insurer
will usually invite renewal of the policy at the end of the period of indemnity. A standard renewal reminder document will be sent to the policyholder. This is an offer (to renew). Tendering the premium will be
acceptance and the contract is then renewed.

The question arises whether the renewal of an existing policy is affected
by the duty to disclose material facts, if there has been a material change in
the risk. Unless the policy specifies that renewal will be automatic, as may
be the case in a life assurance contract, the renewal is in fact a new contract
and both parties are bound by the rules already considered.

In business relations between insurer and policyholder, renewal frequently requires negotiation, but the rules of contract, offer, acceptance and
good faith still apply.

Many renewal invitations contain details of "days of grace". Although
the policy will lapse at the specified date, the insurer may be prepared to
accept the premium a few days, normally two weeks, later. What if the
renewal date passes and a loss occurs prior to payment of the premium
during the days of grace? The rights of the parties vary depending upon
the wording used in the renewal document; each must be looked at individually. One thing is clear, however; if the policyholder has indicated an
intention not to renew the policy, having made it clear that the insurer's
offer to renew is rejected, for example by making a counter offer or attempting to arrange other cover, then the insurer will not be bound by the
tendering of the renewal premium during the days of grace.

# CHAPTER 4

# The theft policy — definitions

## Introduction

It will already have been noted that the words of the theft policy, or any other policy for that matter, do not flow like a narrative. The policy is made up of different parts, all interrelated and having a part to play in explaining the contract terms. Some cross referencing is essential. Each policy begins, however, with the operative clause — the basic promise. (A specimen theft policy is to be found in Appendix E.)

A typical opening clause of a theft policy, setting out the insurer's commitment to the policyholder, reads as follows:

> XYZ Insurance Company Limited (the Insurer) agrees that if during any Period of Insurance
>
> (a) Any of the Property while within the Premises shall be lost or damaged by Theft involving entry into or exit from the Premises by forcible and violent means or
> (b) There shall occur any damage to the Premises falling to be borne by the Insured consequent upon such Theft or any attempt thereat or
> (c) Any of the Property shall be stolen from the Premises consequent upon and in connection with assault or violence or threat thereof to the Insured or any employee of the Insured
>
> Then the Insurer will by payment or at its option by reinstatement or repair indemnify the Insured against such loss or damage to the extent of and subject to the terms and conditions of this policy.

These opening paragraphs are the essential features of the contract. Everything contained in the policy — the conditions, exclusions and the schedule relate to them. It is necessary, therefore, that the insured (potential claimant) understands fully just what the insurer promises to do "subject to the terms and conditions of the policy". Those terms and conditions will be considered in detail later.

## Theft

What then is meant by the word theft? The Theft Act 1968 codified and clarified the law relating to theft and dishonesty in England and Wales. Theft is defined by the Act:

1.  A person is guilty of theft if he dishonestly appropriates property belonging to another with the intention of permanently depriving the other of it; and thief and steal shall be construed accordingly.
2.  It is immaterial whether the appropriation is made with a view to gain, or is made for the thief's own benefit.

Dishonesty is not itself defined, but the Act does attempt to say what is not dishonesty.

Section 2(1). A person's appropriation of property belonging to another is not to be regarded as dishonest;

a.  If he appropriates the property in the belief that he has in Law the right to deprive the other of it on behalf of himself or a third person, or
b.  If he appropriates the property in the belief that he would have the other's consent if the other knew of the appropriation and the circumstances of it, or
c.  (Except where the property came to him as trustee or personal representative) if he appropriates the property in the belief that the person to whom the property belongs cannot be discovered by taking reasonable steps.

The essence of dishonesty is, therefore, one of belief, and it would be for a jury to decide whether or not the defendant really believed he or she had a right to the property. In the context of the theft policy, there could be a situation where, due to a dispute between parties as to ownership of goods, one of them takes the goods (by force or not) from the other. Clearly, this would not be theft if that person believed the goods were his or hers.

The Theft Act 1968 s. 3 (1) proceeds in an attempt to define "appropriates":

Any assumption by a person of the rights of an owner amounts to appropriation. . .

Property is assumed to belong to another if he or she has possession of it or control of it. Appropriation would include taking, destroying, using, selling or pledging — that is, using property as if it were one's own.

The Act reverts to a method of describing what is not "to deprive permanently" in order to explain the final element of theft (s. 6 (1)):

> A person appropriating property belonging to another without meaning the other permanently to lose the thing itself is nevertheless to be regarded as having the intention of permanently depriving the other of it if his intention is to treat the thing as his own regardless of the other's rights . . .

Again, it is for a jury to decide upon the facts whether there was an intention permanently to deprive.

The most common form of dishonestly appropriating a thing without it being theft is the taking of motor vehicles for "joy rides". Hence the need for s. 12 of the Theft Act 1968, Taking a Motor Vehicle or other Conveyance without Authority. There is no intention to deprive permanently and, perhaps most importantly, a motor vehicle owner is easily traced after the vehicle has been abandoned. If the person or persons responsible for taking the vehicle, instead of abandoning it deliberately destroy, paint, or alter or dismantle it, then a jury would presumably have grounds for finding the intention to appropriate the vehicle.

A thief, taking goods from a shop, would have to have a very good story in order to convince a jury that there was not an intention to deprive permanently at the time of the taking, even if the goods were abandoned shortly afterwards.

S. 6 of the Act indicates that intention to deprive permanently is to be assumed if the taker does anything by way of appropriation, even if there is no intention at the time to deprive permanently. Such an appropriation would be the lending of the property in question to another for a long period.

It will have been noticed that the word theft has a very wide meaning. It includes actions which are commonly termed robbery, burglary, stealing and shoplifting among others.

Burglary still has a statutory meaning defined by s. 9 of the Theft Act 1968 and prior to the introduction of the Act, burglary and housebreaking had clear definitions in law. Those definitions are now historical and consideration of them, although interesting, would not assist this text.

It is necessary for the insurer to identify to the insured precisely what aspects of theft fall within the terms of the policy. The promise is that the insurer will indemnify the policyholder if:

(a) Any of the Property while within the Premises shall be lost or damaged by Theft involving entry into or exit from the Premises by forcible and violent means.

## Onus of proof

The first peril insured against, therefore, is theft *involving entry into or exit from the premises by forcible and violent means.*

The onus of proving that a loss was caused by an insured peril falls upon the policyholder. Once the policyholder can present a *prima facie* case, based upon evidence of such a loss, the onus will then shift to the insurer, if the insurer seeks to show that the loss is excluded in some way. Numerous cases have been heard in English courts, and in each, where the policyholder has failed to prove, and the emphasis rests on the word "prove", that the loss occurred as a result of the peril described in the policy, the action has failed.

This burden is demonstrated by the words of Lord Evershed in the Court of Appeal Case of *Regina Fur Company Limited v Bossom* (1958).

> I think that a Defendant — whether he is an underwriter or any other kind of Defendant — is entitled to say, by way of defence, "I require this case to be strictly proved, and admit nothing." Where such is the defence, the onus remains throughout on the Plaintiff to establish the case they are alleging.

Two more recent cases emphasise this point: *Anderson v Norwich Union* (1977) and *Young v Sun Alliance and London Insurance Limited* (1976). In both of these cases, the courts considered whether a loss suffered by the policyholder had arisen as a result of the operation of "storm, tempest or flood" as defined by a "household insurance policy", but from the decisions it can be seen that the judges found themselves bound by the onus of proof resting upon the plaintiff in each case.

## Proximate cause

The use of policy wordings requiring force and violence has been common for many years. The theft policyholder, therefore, must prove that theft has taken place and that the theft was *accompanied by force and violence* during the entry or exit to or from the premises. In other words, it must be shown that the proximate cause of the loss was such a theft.

The doctrine of proximate cause is another aspect of the law relating to insurance which has produced a long list of legal authorities, going back many years.

What is clear from the authorities, is that the law will not follow a train of events forever in search of the original cause of a series of incidents. Each case will be decided upon its facts, whether or not the damage was caused by an insured peril and that will be the occurrence which by direct cause and effect is responsible for the loss.

Extracts from two cases are worthy of note: the judgement in the case of *Lawrence v Accidental Insurance Company Limited* (1881) quoted and agreed with Lord Bacon's *Maxims of the Law* Regulation 1.

> It were infinite for the Law to consider the causes of causes, and their impulsions one of another; therefore, it contenteth itself with the immediate cause . . . therefore, I say according to the true principle of law, we must look at only the immediate and proximate cause of death, and it seems to me impractical to go back ultimately to the birth of the person, for if he had never been born, the accident would not have happened.

A more practical and succinct consideration is found in *Pawsey v Scottish Union and National* (1907):

> the active efficient cause that sets in motion a chain of events which brings about a result without the intervention of any force started or working actively from a new and independent source . . .

So, the cover only applies when force and violence are used to gain entry to or exit from the premises. Damage to internal doors, desks or safes is not enough.

The use of a key, either stolen or a duplicate, is not considered violent, nor is the use of a "skeleton" key. Some losses occur because thieves conceal themselves on premises until the business closes for the day. This, again, is not sufficient, unless the thieves break out of the premises rather than simply undoing a window catch or door bolts from the inside.

The basic rules are contained in short passages from two historic cases and have been considered by the Court of Appeal in a third case in 1989.

In *Re George and Goldsmiths and General Burglary Insurance Association Limited* (1899) the Court of Appeal considered a case where a shop had been left with the door shut but not locked, and someone had entered, broken open a cabinet within and left with goods. The policy covered burglary or housebreaking "by theft following upon actual forcible and violent entry upon the premises . . . " The Court of Appeal decided that the loss had not been accompanied by violent or forcible entry and was not, therefore, covered by the policy.

The rule was considered again in re *Calf and Sun Insurance Office* (1920). An arbitrator had decided for the policyholder and the court heard the appeal. Most of the judgement is today irrelevant to both the Theft Act and modern policy wordings, but Atkin L J said in his judgement:

> I think the view taken by the learned Judges in George's case was this; that by the words "actual forcible and violent entry" it was intended to mean an entry effected by the exercise of force in a manner that was not customary in order to overcome the resistance of the usual fastenings and protections in the premises.

And then:

> If a person turns a key he uses force but not violence. If he uses a skeleton key, he uses force but not violence. If on the other hand, instead of using a key, he uses a pick-lock, or some other instrument or a piece of wire, by which as a lever he forces back the lock, it appears to me that he uses force and violence.

It will be remembered that it is for the insured to prove that the loss was caused by an insured peril. It is not sufficient for the insured to say that he knew the locks and windows and doors were secured, so the thief must have forced the locks back with an instrument. The insured must be able to prove that such is the case. Usually such actions by a thief will leave marks on surrounding woodwork or door fittings. If not, the policyholder will have to provide other proof.

The Court of Appeal considered the recent case of *Dino Services Limited v Prudential Assurance Company Limited* (1989). Thieves obtained keys to the plaintiff's business which had been left in the glove compartment of his car. The car was stolen and when the plaintiff reached his business the next morning, the keys had been used to gain entry and remove property. The insurer refused to pay and the plaintiff brought an action seeking a declaration that he was entitled to be indemnified under the policy. The judge hearing the case upheld his claim on the basis that the unlawful nature of the act committed was sufficient violence to bring a loss within the terms of the policy. The insurer appealed.

The Court of Appeal held that the word "violent" had to be considered according to its ordinary meaning, and meant entry by the use of force which was accentuated or accompanied by a physical act which could be described as violent in nature and character. "Violent" referred to the means of entry and not its unlawful nature.

In giving the judgement the Court of Appeal did seem to be surprised that the parties had accepted that the turning of a key or handle was force, that is, surprised that the earlier cases mentioned above had been accepted as binding authorities. Perhaps if the Prudential had also argued that force was not applied, the Court of Appeal may have agreed with it. However, the point was not raised and the situation for both force and violence remains as outlined in *Calf's* case.

## Damage

Sometimes premises are entered with force and violence, but the perpetrators commit wanton damage. If a thief, having entered with force and violence, then damages a desk or cabinet in an attempt to gain access to it in order to steal, even if nothing is eventually stolen, such damage will fall within the cover afforded by the theft policy, because the proximate cause is theft or attempted theft.

Damage that is deliberate but not connected with any act of theft, for example soiling, graffiti or malicious damage, is not covered by the theft policy even if it is committed by a thief or thieves when on the premises. There may be some instances where it is difficult to separate acts in furtherance of theft and malicious damage, and thus each case must be considered on its merits.

Malicious damage of this sort can be covered by a standard extension to the fire policy. There is no reason why two policies should not operate in respect of one occurrence — that is, if thieves also commit malicious damage as well as damage caused by the act of stealing insured property.

Part (b) of the promise provides additional insurance against damage to the premises caused by any theft as described in part (a), and also against damage caused by attempted theft of the type described in part (a).

The same limitation applies: the damage to the premises must be caused by the peril insured against — theft, as described in the policy, not malicious damage.

Were the theft policy not to provide this cover, the business world would be without insurance, as the standard fire policy, plus the usual extensions, does not include theft damage to the premises.

This part of the promise refers to damage "falling to be borne by the Insured". This means, of course, that the insured must be responsible for the repair either as owner of the premises or by being responsible for repairing such damage under the terms of the lease or other contract.

*Hold up*

Part (c) of the policy provides additional cover for theft committed by what might be termed "holdup".

Thieves who enter premises and attack or threaten to attack the insured or any employee in an attempt to steal are clearly assaulting or threatening to assault or commit violence.

The use of violence to the insured or an employee is easy to comprehend. If the thief or thieves take hold in a threatening way, or strike or attempt to strike, the violence or attempt is clearly shown. But it will be remembered that it is for the insured to prove that the loss took place in a way required by the policy. The insurer may require some evidence beyond an employee saying that violence had been used or threatened. Such evidence could be nervous shock or torn clothing.

It is reasonable to assume that the word "violence" will be interpreted in this context as it was in *Dino's* case — that is by its ordinary and usual meaning, a physical act which can be described as violent in nature.

The act or threat of violence must be aimed at the person present, and violence to an object such as a display case may not be enough. There may be an occasion where the violence displayed even to shop or business fittings is of such ferocity that those present could reasonably fear for their safety and could therefore infer that a threat of violence was being made, and it is suggested that such ferocity would be enough to bring any immediately subsequent and connected loss by theft within this part of the promise.

*Assault and violence*

Assault and violence should be considered in the context of the meaning given to each in criminal law.

Assault is said to be an act by which one person intentionally or wrecklessly causes another to apprehend immediate and unlawful personal violence. (See *Fagan v The Metropolitan Police Commissioner* (1968).)

No contact is necessary for an assault. An assault occurs when one person points a weapon at another, or acts as if a weapon will be used, or perhaps threatens with a fist. This act must be witnessed by the person being threatened otherwise he or she could not "apprehend . . . violence".

The use of violence against a person is considered in cases of battery— the infliction of unlawful personal violence. Violence in criminal law requires only the slightest of blows.

The policy requires theft consequent upon and in connection with assault or violence. Even though such crimes could be proved in a criminal case for the slightest threat or blow, it is suggested that the actions of the insured or employee would have to be reasonable in the circumstances before loss following relatively trivial assault or violence could be accepted as theft within the meaning of part (c) of the policy promise.

For example, a small youth threatening a large adult with a blow from his fist if he were not allowed to leave the premises with insured property would surely not be sufficient.

The policy makes no reference to theft consequent upon and in connection with a threat of violence to an insured's or employee's family not present at the time. Consider the case where the insured's family are taken hostage and the insured is told of that fact in order to persuade him or her to release property from the premises.

If the insured unlocked the premises in the presence of such kidnappers, it is suggested that this must surely be violent and forcible entry as described above.

If the insured was already on the premises and the kidnappers entered without violence and then revealed the hostage situation, could this fall within part (c) of the promise? Probably it would not.

# CHAPTER 5

# The theft policy — indemnity

## Introduction

Indemnity has been mentioned briefly. In the last paragraph of the policy promise it is specifically mentioned.

> ". . . then the Insurer will by payment or at its option by reinstatement or repair indemnify the insured against such loss or damage to the extent of and subject to the terms and conditions of this policy."

The principle of indemnity is fully established within English insurance law; it is strictly enforced and has been since the earliest days of insurance. Brett L J, in the Court of Appeal decision in Castellain v Preston (1893) referred to indemnity as "the fundamental rule" and then went on to say:

> . . . the contract of insurance . . . is a contract of indemnity, and of indemnity only, and that this contract means that the assured in case of loss against which the policy has been made, shall be fully indemnified, but never be more than fully indemnified.

It is also a fundamental rule that if any means exist by which the extent of the loss can be diminished or extinguished other than by the application of the insurance contract, then it must be brought into account before the final amount to be paid under the terms of the policy is calculated. The method of calculating an indemnity, although in the context of a fire, not a theft policy, was given considerable thought in the case of *Reynolds and Anderson v Phoenix Assurance Company Limited and Others* (1978). Mr Justice Forbes in his judgement referred, of course, to *Castellain v Preston*. He then emphasised that an insured should neither be enriched nor impoverished and confirmed the necessity of taking into account wear and tear and betterment.

Another case which emphasised the principal of indemnity, also resulting from a fire, was that of *Leppard v Excess Insurance Company Limited* (1979). In this case, a cottage was destroyed by fire and the insured claimed the cost of rebuilding. It was agreed that the cottage was for sale and evidence was produced to the effect that the vendor Leppard, the insured, would have accepted £4000 immediately before the fire. The Court of Appeal decided that the correct method of settlement would be to pay the market value less the residual value of the land, as this amount represented the loss which had actually been sustained.

An extract from one further legal decision is worthy of note, namely *Burnand v Rodocanachi, Sons and Co* (1882):

> The general rule of law (and it is obvious justice) is that where there is a contract of indemnity (it matters not whether it is a marine policy or a policy against fire on land or any other contract of indemnity) and a loss happens, anything which reduces or diminishes that loss reduces and diminishes the amount which the indemnifier is bound to pay . . .

The basic principles are, then, as follows:

(a) The insured can only be indemnified, that is receive payment, for the intrinsic value of the material loss sustained, and sentimental losses or loss of profits can not play a part. Indemnity fixes the maximum amount payable. If the policy specifies other limits or an excess to be borne by the policyholder, the amount payable for any claim is so reduced.

(b) If the damage to the property insured is partial, the amount payable is the cost of repairing the damage sustained, less an appropriate allowance for wear and tear and betterment. There are no legal authorities which allow the insured to claim a total loss and abandon the damaged property to insurers, but the policy conditions, which will be considered later, prevent such actions.

(c) The insured can only recover the loss once. It does not matter that there may be more than one policy covering the interest of the insured. The question of contribution between policies providing insurance cover for identical interests is considered later (see "Policy condition relating to other insurances").

# Cost of replacement

If property is lost or damaged beyond economical repair the actual replacement cost to the insured at the time of the loss must be calculated. Each insured will have different circumstances to be taken into account. The cost of replacement would include the insured's purchase price, delivery costs to the insured, and the value of any processing charges incurred by the insured up to the time of the loss.

Where VAT has been paid by the insured and is not recoverable from Customs and Excise, then this cost would also be included as it becomes an intrinsic part of the value as part of the purchase price.

In some common law cases, judgements have been given awarding damages based upon replacement costs without taking wear and tear into account. See *Harbutts Plasticine v Wayne Tank* (1970), where damages were awarded in respect of repairs to a building, and *Bacon v Cooper (Metals) Ltd* (1982) where damages were awarded for the cost of replacing a damaged motor in a machine. It should, however, be noted that in each case there were special circumstances applying.

Other principles apply to actions for damages arising from a tort as in these cases; for example, the requirement that the tortfeasors must take their victims as they find them. Indeed there is no evidence that courts considering matters arising from contracts of indemnity have taken the above mentioned cases as authorities.

# Repair or reinstate

As well as indemnifying the policyholder by a cash payment, it will have been noted that the final paragraph of the policy promise retains for the insurer the right to elect to repair or reinstate. This option is of considerable importance in the fire policy where substantial damage to premises is more likely. It is of limited importance to the theft insurer.

However, it does enable the theft insurer to pay a lesser sum than the apparent full value to the insured if the loss can be made good by the insurer for a lesser sum. For example, the insurer may have a facility whereby a discount is available to it from a repairer or supplier of the type of property damaged or lost. In that event, the insurer may elect to instruct that repairer or supplier.

The insurer must elect to exercise this option within a reasonable time.

Once committed to a settlement of a claim by way of a payment, the insurer cannot then change the method to one of repair or reinstatement.

Once the election has been made, by express notice or by conduct, leading the insured reasonably to assume that repair or reinstatement is to take place, the insurer cannot then withdraw. If it transpires that the cost of repair or reinstatement exceeds the value lost or exceeds even the sum insured, the insurer is still obliged in contract to complete the repair or reinstatement.

Indeed, if the insurer, once having made the election, fails to complete its obligation under the contract, or the repair or reinstatement is unsatisfactory, it will be liable to pay damages (see *Brown v Royal Insurance Company* (1859)):

> The Defendants are bound by their election, and if the performance has become impossible, or (which is all they have shown) more expensive than they had anticipated, still they must either perform their contract or pay damages for not performing it.

Clearly, therefore, only in exceptional circumstances will the theft insurer make this election to repair or reinstate and not make a cash payment.

# CHAPTER 6

# The theft policy —
# limits and exclusions

## Introduction

The usual format of the theft policy, once having stated the insurer's promise, proceeds under the headings "Limits", "Exclusions" and "Conditions"; that is policy sections where the insurer identifies the limits to the policy benefits and the duties of both insurer and insured.

As the insurer is, under those headings, limiting to some extent the benefits of the promise made and imposing obligations on the insured, it is appropriate to consider the strength given by law to the words used. That is a consideration of the legal rules governing the construction of the policy, indeed of any contract.

Many cases have been decided and the decisions in those cases enable us to identify the general principles which must apply to all interpretations of contracts. For a detailed analysis, it is recommended that the reader consults *General Principles of Insurance Law* by E R Hardy Ivamy.

The following general principles apply:

(a) The intention of the parties must prevail. This does not mean that one or more of the parties to a contract can successfully argue that their intention was different from what the actual words in the contract say. This principle only applies when the contract is not clear.

(b) The whole of the contract must be considered and not just one particular clause or section.

(c) Written words, either in handwriting or typewriting, will be given more effect than words printed in the document. That is if words added to a preprinted document conflict with the preprinted words, it will be assumed that the added words reveal the true intent of the parties. See *Robertson v French* (1803) particularly the words of Lord Ellenborough:

The only difference between policies of assurance and other instruments . . . is, that the greater part of the printed language of them being invariable and uniform, has acquired from use and practice, a known and definite meaning, and that the words super-added in writing . . . are entitled nevertheless, if there should be any reasonable doubt upon the sense and meaning of the whole, to have greater effect attributed to them than to the printed words . . .

(d) Ordinary rules of grammar are to be applied to a contract, but if the words, even if they are ungrammatical, clearly give the intention of the parties, then any incorrect grammatical construction will be ignored.

(e) Words are usually to be construed according to their normal usage. In *Leo Rapp Limited v McClure* (1955) it was held that goods which were insured against theft "whilst in a warehouse anywhere in the United Kingdom" were not covered whilst in a lorry in an open but locked compound.

Examples relevant to the Theft Policy include:

(i) "gold" has included gold coins;
(ii) "goods" does not mean wearing apparel or personal possessions;
(iii) "iron" does not include steel.

(f) Words which have a particular meaning by known usage of trade will be deemed to have that same meaning in any contract between parties who would all be expected, reasonably, to know and use the word in the same context (see *Robertson v French* (1803)).

(g) Technical legal words must be construed according to their exact technical legal meaning. A word defined in law, for example "riot", will be interpreted to mean the very thing defined in law unless, that is, the contract specifically provides otherwise (see *London and Lancashire Fire Insurance Company v Bolands* (1924)).

(h) The meaning of a word may be limited by, or ascertained from, the context (the rule of *ejusdem generis*); see *King v Travellers Insurance Association* (1931), where a policy required jewellery, watches, field glasses and other fragile or specially valuable articles to be separately declared and valued. The policyholder lost a fur coat. Rowlatt J held that:

> The question I have to ask myself is whether furs are specially valuable articles in the same sort of sense as jewellery, watches, field glasses and cameras are fragile or specially valuable articles. I think that is the modern and plain English translation of the doctrine of Ejusdem Generis. In other words, are they specially valuable articles in the sense exemplified by the particular instances named? That is the natural way of putting it. I do not think they are. Furs are a commonplace article of dress in the case of nearly every woman of any sort of comfortable means at all.

Where there is ambiguity, a reasonable construction will be presumed where possible. The principles mentioned above can be applied in an attempt to do so. Where, however, a reasonable construction cannot be presumed because of the ambiguity, the words used will be construed against the party to the contract that created the document (the rule of *contra proferentum*). So far as insurance is concerned, therefore, any ambiguity in a policy document will be construed against the insurer because the insurer will have prepared the policy document (see the Court of Appeal case of *English v Western* (1940). The ambiguity must be real not fanciful (see *Alder v Moore* (1960)).

Occasionally insurers may accept policy and endorsement wordings drafted by an insurance broker. The legal position is that the insurance broker is usually the agent of the insured, but when issuing cover notes or collecting premiums the broker is the agent of the insurer.

In the event of a dispute arising on the meaning of a policy or endorsement drafted by a broker each case would have to be considered on its merits. It is suggested, however, that if the insurer agrees wordings in advance and allows a broker to issue a policy then the broker will be the agent of the insurer. If the broker prepares a policy on behalf of a client for the client's special needs and persuades the insurer to accept it, he would then be the agent of the insured.

Finally, in any case of inconsistency, any express term will override an implied term in a contract.

## Limits

The policy limits were mentioned when consideration was given to sums insured shown in the schedule.

This section of the policy is quite simple and straightforward. The sum insured is the maximum amount payable during any one period of insurance for any one item.

The section headed "Limits" then restricts the amount payable by part (b) of the promise to an amount "sufficient to make good such damage", thus serving to exclude additional work necessary because of wear and tear or obsolescence.

Section (b) of the limits section of the policy makes it clear that the total sum insured is the maximum payable by the policy. If, therefore, a total loss of any item shown in the schedule is suffered, and the total sum insured is claimed, the insurer cannot be called upon to pay, in addition, the cost of any building repairs which may be associated with the theft.

The use of the following words

> In the event of loss or damage covered by this Policy the Sums Insured shall forthwith stand reduced by the amount of such loss or damage unless the insurers shall agree on payment of an additional premium to reinstatement of the Sums Insured

makes it clear that the insurer only intends to provide insurance protection for the property *once* for the premium paid. It is suggested that the insurer has therefore calculated the appropriate premium for the risk on the basis that the sum insured is only at risk in total once during any period of insurance. By incorporating the words into the policy, the insurer has the opportunity to reconsider the risk after a loss before agreeing to re-establish cover by restoring the sums insured.

So, if a loss is suffered and a claim paid, the sum insured for the item affected is reduced by the amount paid. If the insured then replaces the stolen property and returns the value at risk to the original level, the remaining sum insured will not be sufficient to give complete protection and as it will be less than the value at risk in the event of a further loss, average will apply!

It is usual, then, for the insured to request that the original sum insured should be reinstated and pay the appropriate additional premium due. An endorsement is necessary to show that the sum insured has been so increased and the additional premium will usually be calculated with due regard to the remaining period of indemnity; that is a *pro rata* premium will be calculated.

If the sum insured is not increased following a loss but nevertheless renewal is requested or invited on existing terms, then the sum insured will return to the original level when the renewal premium is paid and the new period of insurance begins.

It has already been seen that where the insured can show that a loss has occurred for which, *prima facie*, he or she can be indemnified by the policy, the onus then shifts to the insurer to prove that that is not the case, ie to show perhaps that the loss is nevertheless excluded by the policy.

## Exclusions

The clauses within the policy under the heading of "exclusions" identify clearly those losses which are not protected by the policy, whether or not the proximate cause of the loss may fall within the definition of the promise.

Exclusions relate to losses in three general categories:

(a) Losses excluded because legislation has already made provision to protect the insured following financial loss, for example Exclusion 1.
(b) Losses which can be more specifically insured by other policies.
(c) Losses which are more difficult to avoid and control and which should therefore be specifically and carefully considered before cover is granted.

The exclusion relating to "Radioactive Contamination" is found in all policies. Nuclear risks are the responsibility, by virtue of legislation, of Government bodies. All losses connected in any way with radioactivity are excluded from the policy cover:

Radioactive Contamination
a    loss or destruction of or damage to any property whatsoever or any loss or expense whatsoever resulting or arising therefrom or any consequential loss

directly or indirectly caused by or contributed to by or arising from
i     ionising radiations or contamination by radioactivity from any nuclear fuel or from any nuclear waste from the combustion of nuclear fuel
ii    the radioactive toxic explosive or other hazardous properties of any explosive nuclear assembly or nuclear component thereof

The exclusions relating to "War and Kindred Risks" is also to be found in most policies. War losses are also the responsibility of Government bodies:

War and Kindred Risks
any consequence of war invasion act of foreign enemy hostilities (whether war

be declared or not) civil war rebellion revolution insurrection or military or usurped power riot or civil commotion

Riot or civil commotion arising from war or revolution (that is, in the context of the theft policy, for example looting) would clearly be excluded by the exception as such aspects would be included in the exception by virtue of the *ejusdem generis* rule already considered.

Looting during civil unrest in cities in the United Kingdom, the breaking into premises by groups of people with intent to steal, and any subsequent theft would clearly be covered by the theft policy. Losses arising subsequently as a result of unconnected groups or individuals entering the then unprotected premises would not be. There would then, of course, be the problem of identifying when each loss took place, a practical problem for the insured and the claims handler acting for the insurer.

If, however, before the initial break in was committed, certain circumstances prevailed which constituted riot and/or civil commotion, then the proximate cause of the loss would be said to be riot, and all losses occurring once the riot situation arose would be excluded. (Losses arising from riot, provided they are not connected with war or revolution, can be covered by an extension to the Standard Fire Policy available from the insurance market.)

Riot has recently been defined by statute, the Public Order Act 1986, and is said to take place when 12 or more persons who are present together use or threaten unlawful violence for a common purpose and the conduct of them taken together is such as would cause a person of reasonable firmness present at the scene to fear for his or her personal safety.

A standard exception for the theft policy is that relating to "Fire and Explosion". The exclusion relates to loss or damage by either or both, however caused. Loss by fire is, of course, insured by the Standard Fire Policy, and that same policy will also provide protection against losses arising from some explosions. Additional explosion cover can be obtained. This exclusion therefore, avoids duplication of policy cover:

Fire and Explosion
loss or damage by fire or explosion

It is feasible that a thief or thieves could use equipment which incorporates flames (for example oxy-acetylene welding equipment) to gain entry to premises or to overcome internal protections once inside. Indeed, explosions have been used to break open walls, doors and safes. Whilst all other losses arising from theft following such damage would fall to be considered under the terms of the theft policy, the damage caused by flame and explosion would not. The insured would have to approach the fire insurer of the building for indemnity.

The exclusion relating to "Glass" limits the restriction to specific types of glass, ie only plate glass, toughened, laminated or stained glass is excluded. Again, policies specifically providing cover for such glass are available, and the exception avoids overlapping insurance cover. Ordinary sheet window glass is not affected by the exclusion. The words usually used are:

> Glass
> damage to plate toughened laminated or stained glass or any decoration or lettering thereon.

It is usual for a theft policy to exclude losses arising from "connivance". For example:

> Loss or damage
> a   By or with the connivance of any member of the Insured's household or by any employee of the insured or
> b   Occasioned by any person lawfully on the premises.

The purpose of this exclusion is to exclude from the policy losses perpetrated by a person or persons who have special knowledge of the business and/or the business protection. If this were not the case, the risk of loss would be greater and underwriting more difficult with subsequent higher premiums.

It is possible to obtain insurance protection against losses by employees in certain circumstances: for example, fidelity guarantee policies and (see later) the money policy.

Part (b) of this same exclusion does not exclude losses by thieves who enter open premises and hide until everyone has left; that is, it does not exclude losses under part (a) of the promise (provided, of course, the thief or thieves use force and violence to make their exit). Even if the thief or thieves decide only when on the premises to commit an offence, from that moment they would no longer be "lawfully" on the premises and so the exclusion would not apply, provided they use force and violence to make their exit or commit an assault as required by part (c) of the promise.

There is finally the exclusion specifically excluding losses to certain property:

> Loss of or damage to money securities tokens vouchers cheques stamps jewellery

watches furs precious metals precious stones or articles composed of any of them tobacco cigars or cigarettes unless specifically mentioned as insured hereunder.

The intention is to exclude property most attractive to thieves because of value and portability, unless, of course, the insurer's underwriter knew of the presence of such property and its value. If the underwriter is aware and has assessed the risk on that basis, such property would then be included in the description of property in the schedule, hence the importance of disclosure of *all* material facts.

Money should be insured separately under a money policy.

This exclusion, so far as it relates to tobacco, does not overrule the cover provided by Exclusion 2 of the "All Other Contents" clause, that is to the value of £50 kept for the purpose of entertaining.

# CHAPTER 7

# Conditions

## Introduction

As was seen earlier, it is implied by law that certain conditions attach to each policy of insurance.

(a) That the parties act in accordance with the principle of utmost good faith.
(b) That the subject matter of the insurance actually exists when the policy is taken out.
(c) That the subject matter be clearly identified.
(d) That the insured has an insurable interest.

Any other condition which the insurer wishes to apply must be written into the policy.

Most policies do indeed contain conditions, and one of those usually emphasises their importance. For example:

> The due observance and fulfilment of the terms and conditions of this policy in so far as they relate to anything to be done or complied with by the Insured and the truth of the statements in the proposal made by the Insured shall be conditions precedent to any liability of the Insurers to make any payment under this policy.

The burden of proving a breach of condition will always rest with the insurer. In the case of *Bond Air Services Limited v Hill* (1955) an aircraft policy contained a condition requiring the insured to observe all statutory requirements relating to air navigation. Another condition contained "the observance and performance by the insured of the conditions . . . are conditions precedent to the Insured's right to recover". A plane crashed and the insurers argued that the insured had to prove that the condition relating to statutory requirements had been complied with. The decision of the Queen's Bench Division was that it was for the insurer to prove a breach once the insured had shown that a *prima facie* claim existed.

Each condition normally found in an insurance policy will be one of three broad types:

(a) Conditions precedent to the policy; a breach of which will render the policy void from inception.
(b) Conditions subsequent to the policy; those which identify the duties which the insured must perform during the currency of the policy.
(c) Conditions precedent to liability; conditions which relate to a loss.

## Void and voidable

The second and third types of condition render the policy voidable.

A void contract is one which has never had any legal force — that is, it never existed.

A voidable contract is one which can be avoided by the aggrieved party — that is, one of the parties may legitimately claim not to be bound by the terms of the contract.

It has already been seen when warranties were considered that a "condition precedent to liability" has the legal strength of the insurance warranty and goes, therefore, to the root of the contract.

Examples of conditions precedent to the policy are the implied conditions already mentioned earlier in this chapter.

Conditions subsequent to the policy will be conditions relating to the non-alteration of the risk or the assignment of the policy (see below).

Conditions relating to the proof of any loss or arbitration are examples of conditions precedent to liability (see below).

If a breach of condition is shown, it is no defence for the insured to show that the breach arose because it was impossible to comply with the condition (see *Worsley v Wood* (1796)).

In the event of a breach, the insurer can waive the breach either expressly or by conduct.

## Delay

However, if there has been a breach, the insurer is not required to seize upon it and claim benefit from it by avoiding the policy or refusing to pay a claim immediately. Provided any delay does not prejudice the insured, and it is reasonable, it is not evidence of waiver.

See *Allen v Robles: Compagnie Parisienne de Guarantie* (1969). Here, on a motor policy, a condition required notification immediately the insured had knowledge of a claim under the policy and at the latest within five days. In April 1967 there was an accident. The insured notified the insurer in July. In November 1967 the insurer advised the insured party that it would pay personal injury damages only (as required by Road Traffic Acts). The third party suffering property damage sued the insured for losses arising from that property damage and obtained judgement. The insured sued the insurer, arguing that delay to November 1967 was unreasonable and that the notification condition had been waived.

The Court of Appeal held that a delay can be reasonable, and delay would only operate against the insurer if the insured was prejudiced or if delay was so inordinate that it could be taken that liability under the policy had been accepted.

## One contract

The section of most policies concerned with conditions usually has as the first condition or as a heading something very similar to:

> This Policy and the Schedule shall be read together as one contract and any word or expression to which a specific meaning has been attached in any part of the Policy or of the Schedule shall bear such specific meaning where ever it may appear.

This paragraph emphasises and confirms what has already been considered, namely that sections of the contract cannot be considered in isolation but the whole document must be read and considered in its entirety.

## Reasonable precautions

Most insurance policies relating to "accident insurance" will contain a condition requiring the policyholder to take reasonable precautions.

Accident insurance is a very broad and ill defined term normally referring to those insurances which are not related to aviation, marine, life and fire insurance matters. It does, therefore, incorporate policies relating to theft, all risks, money, motor and legal liability matters.

A typical reference to "reasonable precautions" would be:

> The Insured shall take all reasonable precautions for the safety of the Property including
>
> (a)  the selection and supervision of employees
> (b)  the securing of all doors, windows and other means of entrance.

Most legal authorities giving guidance as to the interpretation of such a condition have arisen from disputes on all risks (including transit) policies, or policies relating to legal liabilities.

It has already been seen that where the policy is quite specific, then, without doubt, the intention of the parties is clear. So, with the example above, part (b) must be complied with precisely. All doors and windows and other means of entrance must be secured using the devices which the insurer knew were available as a result of disclosure by the insured and/or enquiries and surveys carried out during negotiations prior to inception of the policy or renewal. Indeed, the insurer may have specified the nature of the devices!

If that is not done, then clearly the insured will be in breach of this particular condition, and it has already been seen above, that conditions identifying what the insured must do or not do, are conditions precedent to liability.

Part (a) of this condition is perhaps more difficult. The authorities which are available follow the general principle of insurance law that "reasonable" must mean reasonable in the circumstances prevailing. Indeed, the insured will have complied with the condition if he or she has been guided by normal trade practices appropriate to the business, provided those trade practices are not obviously unsatisfactory. See *London Crystal Window Cleaning Company Limited v National Mutual Indemnity Insurance Company Limited* (1952) and *Pictorial Machinery Limited v Nicholls* (1940).

Reasonable precautions will be considered again later in the context of the all risks policy.

## Material changes

The next condition to be considered also concerns actions taken by the insured once the policy is in force; that is, a condition subsequent to the policy which will read:

No claim shall be recoverable hereunder

(a) if any material change shall be made in the premises or in the conditions of the risks as existing at the time of acceptance or
(b) if the intrinsic value of the contents of the premises be at any time, materially increased unless in any of such cases, the written consent of the insurers has been obtained.

It will be immediately recognised that this condition reinforces the existing common law rights possessed by the insurer resulting from the duties imposed upon the insured by the principles of utmost good faith, and the rules relating to non disclosure and material facts.

It is suggested that a "material change" would be a change in the premises the nature of which is significant enough to be considered a material fact and warrant notification to the insurer. An example could be if the insured, during refurbishment of the premises, replaced an external door with one less substantial than that installed at the time of acceptance of the risk by insurers.

The "condition of the risk" could perhaps be increased by a substantial increase in the volume and value of stock or materials held or the installation of valuable, portable machinery. Certainly the insurer already has the protection of the average clause, but it may well be that an increase in value of the property insured is so large that a prudent underwriter would require substantially improved protections, for example installation of an alarm system.

The intrinsic value of property can also be significant. The property may be described as including non-ferrous metals and the insurer, following a survey or having asked specific questions, may underwrite on the basis that more valuable non-ferrous metals, for example copper, represent only a small percentage of the overall value. If, then, the insured increases the copper percentage substantially, the intrinsic value of the stock will have been increased, possibly to a material degree.

Once again, it will be a question of fact whether or not the changes are material; that is, whether the changes are sufficient to be considered a material fact for underwriting purposes.

It will be recognised that it is for the insurer to prove a breach of this condition, as any other.

# Right to assign the policy

Another condition frequently found in accident policies concerns the insured's right to assign the policy. For example:

> The interest of the Insured under this policy shall not be assignable except with the written consent of the Insurers.

It has long been recognised that an insured can assign the benefit of a policy, that is enter into a legally binding agreement with a third person to give that third person the financial benefit of any claim. This frequently occurs in life assurance and may occur during mortgage arrangements. The insurer has no control over this process as the insurable interest in the property remains with the insured and the insured continues to be bound by the terms of the policy.

The change of interest condition serves to emphasise the direct relationship between the insured and the insurer. Again, it is a condition which emphasises the common law and contractual position already existing. The insurer has contracted with a particular legal person, and the attributes, or otherwise, of that legal person are material facts. The insurer is entitled to know at all times with whom the contract is made. As insurable interest is peculiar to the insured named in the contract, once that insurable interest is transferred (which would be the only reason for assigning the contract itself), then the insurable interest insured by the policy ceases and so, therefore, the contract will no longer be in force.

Assignment has to be completed before the condition is breached (see *Castellain v Preston*).

Without this change of interest condition, there could be an assignment of a policy by operation of law. Upon the death, bankruptcy or liquidation of the insured, the policy would, by law, devolve upon the personal representatives, trustee in bankruptcy or liquidator as appropriate. The Bankruptcy Act 1914 would allow a trustee in bankruptcy to sue, as trustee of the property, and possibly even sue in his or her own name. The change of interest clause, therefore, requires in all cases where there is an attempt to assign the policy, or where the policy is assigned by law, that the insurer is immediately advised and can then agree or not as to the continuance of the policy. In the case of a voluntary assignment, the insurer can decide whether to enter into a new contract with the assignee, and in the case of assignment by law, appropriate steps can be taken to protect the insurer's interests.

# Action by the insured

A particularly important condition always found in insurance policies is the condition which requires action by the insured in the event of a claim. For example, in a theft policy a condition might be:

Immediately upon having knowledge of any event giving rise or likely to give rise to a claim under the policy, the Insured shall

a. Give notice to the Police and render all reasonable assistance in causing the discovery and punishment of any guilty person and in tracing and recovering the property.

b. Give notice thereof to the Insurers in writing and within 30 days thereafter or such further time as the insurers may allow, deliver to the Insurers a claim in writing and supply such detailed proofs and particulars as may be reasonably required.

In no case shall the Insurers be liable for any loss or damage not notified to the Insurers within 30 days after the event.

It has been previously held that a stipulation in a policy requiring notice of a claim within seven days was not a condition precedent to liability (see *Stoneham v Ocean Railway* (1887)). It was also held in that same case, that the use of the word "condition" relating to that stipulation was not sufficient to make it a condition precedent to liability. It is suggested, however, that as most policy conditions contain within them a statement that all of them are conditions precedent to liability, that the above mentioned case will have no bearing today.

The requirement to give notice to the police, of course, provides some opportunity for the culprits to be discovered and perhaps stolen property to be recovered. The condition requires such action to be taken immediately as, clearly, any delay would prejudice police enquiries.

The insurer also requires immediate notice so that its own enquiries can commence as quickly as possible. A telephone call directly to the insurer or to the insured's agent or broker is the usual method of notification. In the event of a loss, of course, the insured also wishes the claim to be processed quickly and is unlikely to delay notification. The insured must then make a claim in writing, frequently using the insurer's report form.

Often, particularly when a loss is large, it is not possible to formulate a claim immediately or, indeed, within 30 days. In such cases, the insurer invariably allows more time as reasonably required.

The final paragraph of the condition protects the insurer against additional claims being made some considerable time after the loss, perhaps after the insurer has closed the company accounts for the year in question. Provided the insurer has not been unduly prejudiced by delay, losses discovered and claims presented outside the time limits given may be accepted.

The loss itself is usually proved by providing evidence of purchase or acquisition of the items stolen. Provision may be made for the cost of delivery and allowance also made for inflationary trends. In the case of "fashion goods", where the value of ageing stock may have fallen, the insured may recover less than the purchase price. A consideration of the claim process is given later.

## Subrogation

The next condition considered, similarly to some already described above, also emphasises and extends the insurer's common law rights.

In the event of a claim being made against the Insurers under this policy

a.   The Insurers may at any time at its own expense use all legal means in the name of the Insured for recovery of any of the property lost and the Insured shall give all reasonable assistance for the purpose.

b.   The Insurers shall be entitled to any property for the loss of which a claim is paid hereunder and the Insured shall execute all such assignments and assurances of such property as may be reasonably required but the Insured shall not be entitled to abandon any property to the Insurers.

This condition is concerned with the important principle of subrogation which has already been considered. See *Castellain v Preston*, and also *Simpson v Tomson* (1877) in which the judgement contained the following:

. . . the well-known principle of law, that where one person has agreed to indemnify another, he will, on making good the indemnity, be entitled to succeed in the ways and means by which the person indemnified might have protected himself against or reimbursed for the loss.

At common law, subrogation rights attach only when the loss has been paid. The first part of the condition allows the insurer to begin attempts to recover immediately, "to strike while the iron is hot". The insurer cannot, however, make the insured take action in order to reduce the amount payable under the policy. If the policy applies to a loss, the insurer must pay according to the contract. The condition confirms this by making it clear that the insurer will bear the cost of attempting to recover from third parties.

It follows that the insured must do nothing which would prejudice the insurer's rights by way of subrogation. For example, the insured must not absolve a negligent party from liability for any damage done without first obtaining the insurer's permission.

The insurers can only bring an action in the name of the insured so long as the latter is still in existence — see *Smith (Plant Hire) v Mainwaring* (1986). Here, the insurers of plant brought an action in Smith's name to recover money paid to the firm following a loss. However, Smith's (Plant Hire) had been wound up after receiving payment from the insurer and before the action came into court. The Court of Appeal held that as Smith's (Plant Hire) no longer existed, the action could not be brought.

When the insurer exercises subrogation rights, it is almost certain law that those rights must be exercised, including the insured's uninsured losses arising from the same loss (see *Commercial Union Assurance Company v Lister* (1874)). Lister owned a mill and an explosion of gas occurred damaging the mill and contents. The insurance cover was inadequate and, in addition to a shortfall on material damage costs, Lister also sustained a loss of profits. He brought an action against the Municipal Corporation for his uninsured losses only, alleging that the explosion had occurred as a result of the negligence of the servants of the Corporation. Eventually, Lister made a legal undertaking that he would sue for the whole amount of the loss, ie insured and uninsured losses. As the insurance contract has reciprocal obligations, it seems probable that the insurer would have been obliged to have sued for the full amount of the loss in Lister's name had the situation been reversed.

## Cancelling the policy

There is nothing to prevent parties to a contract bringing it to an end by mutual agreement. The insured can also cancel the policy by advising the insurer that the insurance protection is no longer required. In that event, the insurer will frequently calculate an return of the premium already paid, having taken into account expenses.

The insurer will also have a policy condition to enable the policy to be cancelled.

The Insurers may cancel this policy by sending seven days notice by registered letter to the Insured at his last known address and in such event, the Insured shall become entitled to the return of a proportionate part of the premium corresponding to the unexpired Period of Insurance

The words are quite specific and clear; what should be particularly noted, however, is that the insurer may cancel by writing to the insured's last known address, not necessarily the insured's address on the policy or the risk address.

Insurers usually only wish to avail themselves of the right to cancel if information becomes available leading them to believe that non-disclosure or misrepresentation (even innocently) has occurred. They will take action to cancel the policy rather than await a possible claim and dispute their obligation to pay.

## Arbitration

A condition requiring arbitration for disputes arising under the policy is to be found in all accident insurance policies. For example:

If any difference shall arise as to the amount to be paid under this policy (liability being otherwise admitted) such difference shall be referred to an Arbitrator to be appointed by the parties in accordance with the statutory provisions in that behalf for the time being in force. Where any difference is by this condition to be referred to arbitration, the making of an Award shall be a condition precedent to any right of action against the Insurers.

Arbitration arises only where the insurer has agreed that the policy applies to the loss, but the dispute concerns the amount to be paid. The arbitrator is to be appointed by mutual consent and the condition reinforces the statutory requirement that proceedings cannot be commenced in a court until the arbitrator has made an award. In fact, the statutory requirements are quite strict. These requirements are governed by the Arbitration Acts 1950-1979. There can only be a judicial review, that is the matter can only be referred, after arbitration, to the High Court by way of appeal if a question of law arises out of the award. If an arbitrator decides on a question of fact, there can be no appeal on that question of fact.

It is sometimes suggested that arbitration is cheaper than a hearing in courts of law. This may be true where relatively minor losses are concerned, but in more complex cases, where disputes are more likely to arise, it is normal to employ solicitors, barristers and experts to present each party's case to the arbitrator, and so costs are likely to increase, possibly to the level of those likely to be incurred in normal legal proceedings.

However, there are advantages to arbitration. The proceedings are comparatively private, and certainly they are less formal and likely to be completed faster.

## Contribution

The final condition to be considered is that relating to the situation which will arise if there is more than one policy covering the interest in the property insured. This condition is frequently known as the "contribution" condition.

Careful consideration of the insured's needs should ensure that premiums are not paid more than once for the same risk but, from time to time, dual insurance does arise. When this occurs even if the policy did not make provision for contributions from other insurers any insurer making a payment under the policy could still recover an appropriate proportion from the other or others. Indeed, unless the policy provides otherwise, the insured could claim on different policies in any order until such time, of course, as an indemnity had been provided. The right to a contribution from other insurers does not arise from the principle of subrogation; it is an equitable right.

The common law principle of contribution is described in Halsbury's *Laws of England* 4th Edition, Vol. 25, page 285, paragraph 538.

Contribution in the case of over insurance. Subject to any policy conditions to the contrary, the assured may effect as many policies as he pleases; but where the contract is one of indemnity, however numerous the policies may be, he cannot recover more than the total amount of his loss. Most policies of non-Marine insurance contain a contribution clause limiting the liability of the insurers to their rateable proportion of the loss. In this case, the assured cannot claim payment in full under any of the policies; each policy is liable for its rateable proportion only. If there is no such contribution clause in the policy, the assured is entitled to claim payment in full under any of the policies, leaving the insurers under that policy to claim contribution from their co-insurers.

The question of contribution was considered in detail in the case of *North British and Mercantile v The Liverpool London and Globe* (1877). Grain in a warehouse was insured by its owner and the warehouse operator. The grain was damaged by fire and argument arose as to who should pay the loss. Following the judgement in the case, it is now recognised that contribution at common law will not arise except under the following circumstances:

(a) Irrespective of whether the sums insured are different, or other property is insured also, some of the damaged property must be identifiable as "property" within the meaning of both policies.
(b) The loss or damage must be caused by the contingency against which the insurance policy provides cover — for example, loss by theft being covered by both policies or one policy providing theft cover, the other(s) "all risks".
(c) The policies must insure the same interests, ie the insurable interests of the same insured.
(d) The policies in question must, of course, be in force at the time of the loss.
(e) The insurers can, by the wording of their policies, restrict or exclude their rights or duties to contribution.

How then does the theft policy provide for this situation? The following is a typical wording:

If at the time of any loss or damage, there be any other insurance effected by, or on behalf of the Insured, covering any of the Property, the liability of the Insurers hereunder, shall be limited to its rateable proportion of such loss or damage.

If any such insurance is expressed to cover any of the Property hereby insured but is subject to any provision whereby it is excluded from ranking concurrently with this policy either in whole or in part or from contributing rateably to the loss or damage, the liability of the Insurers hereunder, shall be limited to such proportion of the loss or damage as the sum hereby insured bears to the value of the property.

The second part is the easier to analyse. If the other policy (or policies) by their wording ensure that they will not contribute at all to any loss, if another policy is in force, then provided the sum insured on the policy we are here considering is adequate, then any loss will be paid in full. If, however, the other policy (or policies) have been arranged to "top up" the insurance cover to the equivalent of the full value at risk, then the theft policy will only pay a rateable proportion in accordance with the average clause mentioned above.

The first part of the condition being considered is a wording almost universally used today both in fire and accident policies. Its effect is to

ensure that each of the policies in force pay a rateable proportion. Unfortunately "rateable proportion" does not have a legal definition. Insurers have
developed methods of calculating the proportions due under each policy.
The insured having paid his or her premiums, is entitled to recover the
whole extent of the loss provided the combined sums insured are adequate.
Courts would clearly not allow the insurers to make a calculation between
them which would in any way diminish the indemnity payable.

Complications have also arisen when some policies were subject to
average and some were not. Sometimes policies covered the same interest
in the same property, other times policies overlap but cover different
interests in addition to that suffering the loss.

The most complicated method of calculation is known as the "mean
method of apportionment". This was historically applied to calculate contribution arising between non-concurrent, non-average policies. It is sel-
dom used today and as average applies almost universally to theft policies
it is not proposed to give any consideration to this method here.

Concurrent policies are those which provide insurance for the same
interest in exactly the same subject matter. For example, both policies
provide cover for stock. Policies are said to be non-concurrent when the
subject matter is different but overlapping, for example, when one policy
covers stock and the other stock and machinery or, perhaps, stock in two
places (only one of those places being, of course, the same premises as the
first policy).

The easiest method of calculating contributions is known as the sums
insured method of apportionment. As the name implies, the sums insured
on each of the policies are added together and each insurer will pay that
proportion of the loss equivalent to the proportion of the sum insured to
the total sums insured. It is not, however, appropriate where either policy
is subject to average.

For example:

Policy A covers shop contents with a sum insured of £5,000.

Policy B covers the same interest in the shop contents with a sum
insured of £10,000.

The total of the sums insured is therefore £15,000.

A loss of £3000 occurs.

Policy A will pay:

$$\frac{£5000}{£15,000} \times £3000 = £1000$$

Policy B will pay:

$$\frac{£10,000}{£15,000} \quad x \quad £3000 \quad = \quad £2000$$

This method is very simple, but does not take into account complications which might arise when average applies.

The method most frequently used is the "independent liability method" when considering contributions arising under policies which are subject to average. This method was in fact suggested in the case of *North British and Mercantile Insurance Company v London Liverpool and Globe Insurance Company* (1877) to calculate the contributions due from the insurer had the court decided that contributions ought to be made.

Contribution on the basis of the independent liability method is governed by the limits of liability under the policies (the limits of liability, that is, for the concurrent interest only).

For example:

Policy A has a sum insured of £5000 on stock.

Policy B has a sum insured of £10,000 on stock and fixtures and fittings.

Actual value at risk is £8000.

A loss of £3000 is suffered.

Both policies are subject to average.

The independent liability of policy A is:

$$\frac{\text{Sum insured} \quad £5000}{\text{Value at risk} \quad £8000} \quad x \quad \text{(loss) } £3000 \quad = \quad £1875$$

Policy B would have an independent liability of £3000 as average would not operate.

Therefore, total liabilities, ie liabilities of A and B combined, equal £4875.

Thus the calculation of the payments would be based on the respective independent liabilities.

*Policy A*

$$\frac{£1875}{£4875} \quad x \quad £3000 \quad = \quad £1154$$

*Policy B*
£3000

$$\frac{£3000}{£4875} \quad x \quad £3000 \quad = \quad \frac{£1846}{£3000}$$

It is interesting to observe that, when the sums insured by each average policy are independently inadequate to cover the total value but are together adequate, both the sum insured and the independent liability methods produce the same answer.

Agreements between accident insurance offices have been restricted to the settlement of claims arising under non-commercial policies, that is under household, motor and travel policies. That agreement provides for the calculation of contributions to be made on the basis of the independent liability method, confirming its fairness and efficiency.

Sometimes the insured is required to bear a part of any loss, that is an "excess" operates to reduce the amount payable. The independent liability method of calculation will, of course, incorporate the application of the excess when calculating the independent liability of the policy concerned.

# First loss or partial value policy

It can reasonably be argued by some insureds that the size and nature of their business make it impossible for more than a relatively small proportion of the property to be lost by theft on any one occasion.

Consider a large retail department store or warehouse. The value of the property within will be many millions of pounds sterling, and loss by theft could not possibly amount to more than a fraction of the full value. The question then arises whether such businesses should insure for the full value at risk and have premiums based upon that full value in order to avoid the application of average in the event of a loss.

In such instances, the insurer will be prepared to issue a "first loss" or "partial value" policy. The policy will be issued with a sum insured less than the full value at risk (usually not less than 20%), representing the maximum likely loss on any one occasion. Premium calculations are complex and specially worded average clauses may apply. These policies are specifically arranged for each individual insured's requirements. A typical average clause would be:

If the declared value of the property covered hereby be less than the actual value at the time of destruction of or damage to such property by any peril hereby insured against, the amount payable shall be proportionately reduced.

Similar problems are encountered by businesses with fluctuating values at risk, particularly where property is held in more than one place. These problems can be overcome by the use of "stock declaration policies". Such policies will also overcome any difficulties which may have been encountered by losses having the effect of reducing the sum insured.

Premiums are based upon declarations of actual value at risk made by the insured on a monthly or quarterly basis. A provisional premium is payable initially, the sum insured being established at the likely maximum value at risk during the year. At renewal an adjustment is made based upon the average of the values at risk declared during the year.

These policies are still subject to average and if a declaration is not made to the insurer when it should be, the policy usually provides that the maximum value of the sum insured will be taken as the declared value for the date in question.

The policy usually provides for automatic reinstatement of the sum insured after a loss and for the payment of a *pro rata* premium for the reinstated value at risk.

Stock declaration policies are suitable for warehousing businesses where there is a potential large variation in stock value related to deliveries "in" and "out".

## Agreed value

The nature of stock held by some businesses may promote difficulties in arriving at a true indemnity in the event of a loss. Gem stones can fluctuate wildly in value, and secondhand but valuable property (for example antiques) is difficult to value at the best of times. In appropriate circumstances, the insurer will usually be prepared to issue a "valued" or "agreed value" policy.

The policy will incorporate a clause to the effect that the sum insured has been accepted by the insurer and insured at the true value of the property and that in the event of a loss, the property will be assumed to be of such value.

Difficulty may be encountered still, however, in the event of a partial loss. The principle of indemnity still applies, and in the event of a partial loss, an agreement must be reached between the parties. A guide as to how this should be done is found in the case of *Elcock and Others v Thomson* (1949).

A building with a sale price of £18,000 was insured with an agreed value in excess of £100,000. A fire occurred, but the building was not totally destroyed, even though the cost of rebuilding exceeded the pre-fire sale value. Even when damaged, the market value of the building was said to be approximately two thirds of its pre-fire value.

The fire damage repairs were not carried out and the court had to decide what was the appropriate indemnity. The decision was that the percentage of the reduced market value would be applied to the total "agreed value" sum insured.

It should be fully appreciated that a valued policy where the indemnity value is agreed at the time of arranging the cover and not when the loss occurs, is *totally* different from the situation where an item to be insured is simply valued and the sum insured fixed accordingly. In this second case the valuation is only a method of establishing an appropriate sum insured. It is no different from the process of establishing the sum insured for which a building or machinery should be insured. Given possible wide variations in the value of gold, for example, it is very possible, indeed probable, that a bracelet could be valued and a sum insured established as the valuation amount but six months later the actual value of the bracelet might be much more or much less than the original valuation and thus the sum insured would be too low or too high. This is a problem more usually found in all risk covers.

# CHAPTER 8

# The money policy

## Introduction

The money policy is frequently placed in the class of insurances called "all risks". Like all such policies, this is a misnomer. All risks should be taken to mean insurance cover relating to all accidental loss or damage but with certain restrictions. Restrictions usually placed on such policies are normally associated with policy cover available elsewhere, for example fire and fidelity guarantee policies, together with risks which would not normally be protected by insurance cover, namely pilfering and shortages arising from errors and omissions. (There is a specimen money policy in the Appendix.)

## Operative clause

As in all policies, the operative clause or promise is the basis or foundation upon which the other elements of the contract are placed.

A typical money policy operative clause would be:

The Insurers agree that during any Period of Insurance, in the event of

a. Loss of Money
b. Loss of, or damage to
   i   Safe or strong room
   ii  Case, bag or waistcoat when such is used for the carriage of Money

Directly associated with any theft or attempted theft therefrom except in so far as this cost is otherwise insured.

c. Loss or damage to clothing and personal effects being sustained by the

Insured or any partner, director or employee of the Insured as a result of an assault by a person or persons attempting to steal money.

Occurring in the situations the Insurers will indemnify the Insured against such loss or damage to the extent of and subject to the terms and conditions of this Policy.

## Definitions

The meaning of the words "period of insurance" has been considered earlier. "Money" is defined in the policy. Indeed the policy definition includes not only cash and bank notes (British and non British) but also any documents which can be readily changed into money or which are the equivalent of money: for example postage stamps and National Insurance and savings stamps.

A typical definition would be:

Cash Bank and Currency Notes Cheques Girocheques Postal and Money Orders Crossed Bankers Drafts Premium Bonds Saving Certificates Stamps Unexpired Units in Franking Machines National Insurance Stamps National Savings and Holidays with Pay Stamps Luncheon Vouchers Credit Card Sales Vouchers Trading Stamps Gift Tokens Consumer Redemption Vouchers and VAT Purchase Invoices.

It will be seen that a number of vouchers and invoices are also included. However, it will also be seen that these are, so far as a business is concerned, the equivalent of cash, each being readily changed for cash or cash value, during normal trading.

VAT stands for, of course, Value Added Tax. This is a tax collected by Customs and Excise after it has been charged on each added value transaction. The supplier to, for example, a shop proprietor, would provide an invoice for goods purchased by the shop proprietor and add the appropriate percentage of VAT (at the time of writing this is 15%).

The shop proprietor, when selling the property so supplied, would also add to his or her sales price the same proportion of VAT. He or she would then be holding that amount of tax for Customs and Excise. By way of periodic returns (currently every three months), the proprietor in this example would make a declaration to Customs and Excise showing the amount of VAT paid by him or her to suppliers and deducting that tax from the amount collected from customers. The balance is the amount that the shop proprietor would have to pay, quarterly, to Customs and Excise.

It will be seen that if VAT invoices are stolen, the proprietor will not be able to indicate in the quarterly declaration the amount of VAT which has already been paid to suppliers. That being the case it will not be possible to offset that amount already paid against the amounts added to his or her own sales. The proprietor will, therefore, be required to pay the total amount of VAT collected by him or her but without offsetting the amounts already paid. The VAT invoices are, therefore, as valuable as cash to the proprietor in this example.

The proprietors of companies providing trading stamps, gift tokens and similar documents may well have an insurance scheme providing cover in the event of loss of such documents, even though the contract between the parties does not provide for immediate reimbursement. In such circumstances, it is common for the respective insurers to share the loss, calculating contributions by the "independent liability" method.

The meaning of the word "loss" is of prime importance. Money, as defined by the policy, can be lost in many ways.

The most final of such losses could be where money as defined by the policy is destroyed by fire or accident. Is it even then lost, however? Cash which is totally burnt or destroyed is certainly lost. The value of credit card sales vouchers would also be lost in such circumstances, as would postage stamps and other items which are not individually recorded.

Savings certificates and premium bonds may have the true owner recorded by the relevant official office and credit could thus be obtained. The same may apply with vouchers (see above).

In the event of cheques being destroyed, it is probable that a business will be able to identify the items so destroyed by reference to invoices and, having persuaded the cheque presenter that the original has been lost, the insured should also be able to obtain a fresh one.

Money as defined by the policy can also be lost by theft. Cash and easily negotiable non-traceable documents will surely be lost immediately they are stolen unless, of course, the thief is apprehended in a very short period of time. The vouchers will be very difficult to convert to cash and will probably be destroyed by the thief or thieves. The insured would have to act very quickly to contact cheque presenters to ensure that each one arranges for stolen cheques to be stopped by the appropriate bank. In the event of that action being unsuccessful and a cheque being fraudulently banked, then the insured would certainly have lost the value of the cheque or cheques. A reasonable time must be allowed to elapse in order to ascertain the true loss.

What if money, as defined by the policy, is mislaid? If it is lost in transit away from the premises, then the same considerations as outlined above will apply. Money, as defined, will surely be returned to its rightful owner in a short space of time if it has been found by an honest person. It can be assumed to be lost for the purposes of the policy after a reasonable time has elapsed. What is a reasonable time would, of course, depend upon the specific circumstances of each incident.

There can be cases where the insured does not know where the money, as defined, has gone! If it has gone missing whilst within the premises, then theft is usually assumed. There are other possibilities of course; it may have been inadvertently thrown away. It is suggested that most insurers will follow the decision of *Holmes v Payne* (1930) where it was held that an item was lost if it could not be found after a diligent search and a reasonable period of time.

The word "loss" in the policy means irretrievably lost to the insured, and in each case a decision will have to be made based upon the facts available: that is, the nature of the loss, the nature of money as defined, and the period of time which has elapsed since the loss was discovered.

Part (b) of the promise follows the format of the theft policy in relation to damage caused to premises by theft or attempted theft. What constitutes a safe or strong room would be taken from normal trade considerations. The proviso concerning cost of repair being otherwise insured brings into question, once more, the overlapping of cover, possibly with theft or fire policies.

If damage has been caused by the use of equipment producing flames, then the fire policy may apply. If a separate theft policy is in force, then the cost of repairing safe and strong rooms will normally be shared by the policies, each contribution being calculated by the independent liability method considered earlier in Chapter 7.

The money policy will carry a condition relating to other insurances. A typical wording would be

> If at any time of any loss or damage, there should be any other insurance effected by or on behalf of the Insured covering the same loss or damage, the liability of the Insurers shall be limited to its rateable proportion of such loss or damage.

The fire policy (or other policy) mentioned above will almost certainly have a condition with identical meaning. It has already been seen, when the question of contribution was considered, that even if such conditions are not present in the policies, the law would still require a calculation of rateable proportions because of joint insurance of the same insurable interest.

The second part of part (b) of the promise concerns the loss of the item in which money (as defined) is carried. Of course, any case or bag or waistcoat could be used to carry money, but some are specially designed for such a purpose and, being specially designed and specially made, they can be very expensive. The use of the carefully designed waistcoats, like money belts, is to disguise the fact that quantities of cash might be being carried.

Part (c) of the promise is clearly worded and the nature of the cover has already been considered when examining the theft policy.

## Territorial limits

The next section normally found in the money policy is that relating to the situation or territorial limits.

Money policies vary considerably in the method used to describe where losses are covered by the policy and the extent to which the insurers limit their liability in each particular circumstance and situation.

The intention is to provide policy cover in a wide range of circumstances and situations but to an extent in each case, reflecting a reasonable limit of liability.

Most policies will provide cover for situations

. . . within Great Britain, Northern Ireland, the Republic of Ireland, Channel Islands and the Isle of Man.

The additional restrictive circumstances may then be outlined in the policy with those same situations and circumstances repeated again in the schedule, showing against each the limit of liability of the insurer. Alternatively, the policy refers directly to the schedule to describe the circumstances, situations and limits together.

For this reason, it is impossible to provide a typical wording for this part of a money policy. However, in a variety of ways, cover will normally be provided by the use of various words for the following:

(a)  whilst in transit;
(b)  in bank night safes;
(c)  at the insured's business premises specified in the schedule;

(d) at any of the insured's sites of contract;
(e) in private residences of the insured or a director, partner or employee of the insured.

If the words "in transit" are used, this will mean, of course, that cover applies whilst money, as defined, is being carried from one place to another. This will usually be from one of the places described in the situation to another, but not necessarily so. It may be that an insured or employee is required to carry cash for business purposes whilst trading from one place, for example a market, to another. The fact that money is being carried in this way almost constantly would be a material fact, but provided the insurer was aware of it and of the quantities involved, then the money being so carried would be protected by the words "in transit".

If the words "in bank night safe" were used, the meaning is quite straightforward. Most banks provide a night safe facility, so that money with supporting documentation can be placed into the premises out of banking hours and be safely kept until they open for business and accept responsibility for the money.

The banks will accept responsibility for money once it is in their possession — that is, once it has been handed over the counter at their premises. Thus, if in the process of an armed bank raid, money was taken from customers standing in the reception area, as well as being demanded from and released by bank staff "over the counter", the money taken from the customers in the reception area would be at their own risk; that is, for the purposes of the money policy it would be in transit.

Banks do not normally accept responsibility for money in night safes until it has been removed and checked against the paying in slip. The money policy providing cover in bank night safes will therefore provide insurance protection to the insured until that moment.

*Business hours*

When providing cover during business hours, the money policy will provide cover "in the premises specified in the Schedule during Business Hours".

What constitutes the premises has already been considered in the section considering the theft policy.

The money policy defines "business hours" either in the policy itself or the schedule. The wording almost universally used is as follows:

The period during which the Insured's Premises or Sites of Contract are actually occupied for business purposes and during which the Insured or any director partner, or employee of the Insured entrusted with money is in the Premises or at Sites of Contract.

Two requirements are identified by this definition. The premises or sites must be actually occupied for business purposes, that is business as described in the schedule (see reference to "The Business" during the consideration of the theft policy). In addition, the person entrusted with the money must be present. A clear example of this can be seen if a representative of the insured visits a contract site to pay wages to employees working there. The wages would be protected by the money policy provided the person responsible for taking the wages there and distributing them was present on the contract site. If he or she left the wages at the contract site without there being particular arrangements for someone else to take over responsibility for the money, cover would cease.

A typical wording providing cover outside business hours is as follows:

In the Insured's premises out of business hours

a    Secured in locked safe or strongroom
b    Not secured in locked safe or strongroom

What constitutes business hours has been considered above.

What constitutes a safe or a strongroom can only be that which is accepted as such by the manufacturers of the items and by general usage. There is no legal definition of a safe or a strongroom.

It will be easily imagined that such items do, therefore, vary considerably with regard to efficiency and strength. A cheap, fairly lightweight free-standing safe will provide very little protection. The heavier, more substantially constructed and, therefore, more expensive safe will provide greater protection. A well constructed strongroom will no doubt provide the best security.

It will be seen below that insurers limit their liability out of business hours. It may be that a particular insured needs to keep large quantities of money on the premises out of business hours. In that event, the insurer will need to know, if not to specify, the nature of the safe and/or strongroom used and will, by way of negotiation, agree specific limits of liability appropriate to the safe or strongroom available.

Before an insurer would be persuaded to increase its usual limits of liability out of business hours, it would normally have to be satisfied that money was kept in a safe weighing more than one ton or one that is at least permanently fixed to the structure of the building.

Normally, a substantially lower limit of liability will be provided for cash out of a safe out of business hours.

Finally, cover is available for cash in private residences. A typical wording might be:

> In the residences of the Insured or any partner, director or employee of the Insured.

No further comment as to the meaning of that phrase is warranted here.

## Limits of liability

It was mentioned above that the insurer will apply different limits of liability to each circumstance or situation described in the policy.

This is normally done in the policy schedule. An example of a schedule is to be found in the Appendix and it will be seen there that the limits of liability of the money policy are not only restricted to different situations, but also vary according to the nature of the money as defined. The first part of the schedule relating to limits of liability will refer to: "Bank notes, currency notes, uncrossed bankers' drafts, uncrossed postal orders, uncrossed money orders, uncrossed cheques".

The schedule then identifies each limit of liability by reference to losses:

(a)  during business hours (as described above);
(b)  out of business hours;
(c)  in private residences.

It may also specifically mention transit.

Limits of liability for each of those situations will be relatively low. There are very few businesses which need to hold large quantities of cash or easily negotiable documents. The insurer will attempt to allocate limits under each situation appropriate to the business in question and to the needs of the business as outlined in the proposal form or negotiations.

Those businesses which do hold large amounts of cash, for example supermarkets, would certainly need higher levels of indemnity, but would also have to satisfy the insurer that there was an efficient and well organised system for controlling the presence of cash at any one point and transferring all cash to safe points at regular intervals.

It should be particularly noted that the money policy does not carry an average clause. In the event of under insurance, the amount payable will not be proportionately reduced. However, if, upon enquiry, it transpires that the cash at risk consistently and significantly exceeded the agreed limits of liability, then the insurer may be able to show that the regular holding of additional cash was a material fact, and that the insured had been guilty of non-disclosure with, of course, the consequences considered earlier.

It is because individual insured's needs vary that the limits of liability section of the schedule will have amounts appropriate to each individual insured.

For the same reason, the insurer will decide upon an appropriate limit of liability for any safe used for the storage of money as defined, out of business hours.

Money not in a safe out of business hours or in private residences is unlikely to be protected to any great extent. The limits of liability are, therefore, frequently printed in the schedule at relatively modest levels. £500 is a commonly used limit and it is unlikely that an insurer would provide cover beyond £1000 at the time of writing.

Some businesses have connected to or incorporated within the premises a private residence. For example, shops, public houses and hotels. In such an event, difficulties could arise where money as defined, that is belonging to the business, is stolen during business hours but from the part of the building used as a private residence.

If, in the schedule, the premises are described as "occupied by the Insured as [for example] public house and dwelling", then the limit of liability applicable during business hours must apply to the private residence portion also.

If the premises are described in the schedule as (for example) "public house", then the limit of liability for "money in residences of the Insured etc" will apply to any loss from the private residence portion, whether during business hours or not. This limit is, as already seen above, a relatively modest amount.

The second part of the schedule will normally show the limit of liability applicable to money not described in the first part; that is, money as defined consisting of:

Crossed cheques, crossed Giro cheques, crossed Banker's drafts, crossed money orders, National Savings certificates, premium bonds, credit and sales vouchers and VAT purchase invoices.

The limits applicable will be fairly generous and it will be seen that the insured will be indemnified for losses anywhere in the situation; that is, the limits relating to business premises, etc do not apply. The reason for this is, of course, that the possibility of a substantial loss can be greatly reduced by positive action by the insured and by the difficulty of obtaining cash benefit to the detriment of the insured by any finder or thief.

Finally, the limits of liability section of the policy or schedule will usually make clear the extent to which the policy will reimburse the costs of repairing damage done to safes, strongrooms or clothing. Usually, in the case of safes and strongrooms, the cost of repair or replacement without limit will be included.

# CHAPTER 9

# The money policy — exclusions

There are three exclusions usually found in the money policy which are unique.

## Dishonesty of employees

A typical wording is:

> This policy does not cover any loss arising from fraud or dishonesty of any employee of the Insured
>
> a.  Unless discovered within seven working days after its occurrence
> b.  Covered by a policy of fidelity guarantee insurance.

It must first be remembered that this being a money policy, losses referred to by this exception, can relate only to losses of money as defined.

Financial losses suffered by the insured as a result of stock manipulations or pilfering are simply not covered by the money policy, whether or not a policy of fidelity guarantee applies.

For the money policy to apply, the actions of the employee(s) must, in this example, be discovered within seven working days of any individual occurrence. In the event of a single theft, this is not a problem, but losses arising from the activities of dishonest employees are frequently ongoing and are not discovered for some time. The most common dishonest act by an employee is known as "teaming and lading". Usually the employee begins by borrowing cash intending to replace it on pay day. Once in the habit, the amount involved grows and replacement becomes difficult. The employee then replaces the shortfall with other incoming cash or by moving cash or cash deposits, concealing the deceit by simple book entries and delayed banking. Frequently, the amount involved increases and control by the dishonest employee becomes impossible, even if the deceit has not already been discovered by normal auditing methods. This kind of loss is not protected by the money policy. That policy will only provide for reimbursement of any money as defined taken within the last seven working days, or other period specified by the exclusion.

*Fidelity guarantee policy*

In order to provide protection against this and other "pilfering" type frauds, employers can obtain the benefit of a fidelity guarantee policy. In this event the exclusion in the money policy will exclude all money losses, but there is no reason, of course, why the fidelity guarantee policy should not exclude losses discovered within seven working days of each occurrence so that there is thus no overlap of cover.

# Errors

The next exclusion usually found on the money policy is unrelated to dishonesty of employees: "Shortages due to error or omission".

This exception excludes apparent financial losses incurred by the insured which have arisen as a result of trading practices or errors of accounting, ie there is no actual physical loss of money as defined.

# Loss from unattended vehicle

Many money policies carry the exclusion "loss from an unattended vehicle".

What is meant by unattended? If money as defined is left in a vehicle, locked or otherwise, and the driver and other occupants leave the vehicle totally out of sight, then it must be unattended and no cover will attach. It is interesting that this one exception has produced a number of legal authorities.

In *Donohue v Harding* (1988) the circumstances of loss were that a driver left his vehicle near to a petrol station kiosk whilst he paid for petrol. Although he was within the kiosk, he could see the vehicle and had locked it. Whilst paying for the petrol, a thief crept behind the vehicle and opened the door with a duplicate key. It was held that the vehicle was attended, because it was considered that the driver had a reasonable prospect of preventing any interference or of raising an alarm.

In *Ingleton v General Accident* (1967), a driver left his vehicle for 15 minutes whilst making a delivery. Although he could see the vehicle, he was considered to have been too far away to have prevented unauthorised access. It was held that the vehicle was unattended.

In *Plaistow Transport v Graham* (1966), the driver was asleep inside the vehicle and, perhaps quite rightly, it was held that the vehicle was attended.

The most authoritative case is *Starfire Diamond Rings Limited v Angel* (1962). A jeweller left his vehicle at the roadside and walked 40 yards away, leaving jewellery inside the vehicle. The Court of Appeal considered the case and decided that the ordinary meaning of the word "unattended" must be applied. "Attended" then implies two things:

(a) the vehicle must be under observation in order that any attempted interference can be seen and

(b) the attendant should be close enough to have a reasonable prospect of preventing unauthorised interference.

In this case, the driver of the vehicle had, in fact, lost sight of it whilst he rounded some bushes, and it was held that the vehicle was not attended.

injury and which injury shall independently of any other cause be the sole cause.

# CHAPTER 10

# The money policy — extension

## Personal assault or accident

The money policy has a personal assault or accident extension. The intention is to pay the insured certain benefits if he or she or a partner, director or employee of the insured suffers either death or permanent disablement. The benefits payable are specified by the policy, but it is important to note that they are payable to the insured and not to the injured person if that is not the insured.

A typical extension begins

the Insurer agrees that if as a result of an attempt by thieves to steal

1. Money Insured
2. Stock in trade belonging to the insured from the Premises whilst such Premises are open for business . . .

It will be seen from this opening that the extension applies to almost any situation where someone is injured in an attack to steal money, but in addition it extends to provide insurance cover when the theft or attempted theft is of stock in trade and not money alone.

### Bodily injury

The extension then continues

The Insured, or Partner, Director or Employee of the Insured shall suffer bodily injury and which injury shall independently of any other cause be the sole cause of death or disablement as hereunder the Insurer will pay to the Insured or his legal personal representatives, the Compensation specified in the schedule for any of the Results specified below.

The important consideration here is the meaning of the words "bodily injury which . . . shall independently of any other cause, be the sole cause of death or disablement . . . ".

Bodily injury is a simple concept. Cuts, bruises, broken bones and dislocations are bodily injury; shock, fright or a nervous reaction *are not*.

*Proximate cause*

The use of the words "independently of any other cause", is a particular reference, of course, to proximate cause. The principle of proximate cause is equally important in personal accident insurance; indeed, many of the legal authorities have arisen as a result of claims under that type of policy. The death or disability must have been caused directly by the assault and no new intervening causes must have an effect (see *Pawsey v Scottish Union and National*, already discussed).

In *Etherington v Lancashire and Yorkshire Accident Insurance Company* (1908–10), a rider fell from a horse and as a result of lying without aid died of pneumonia. The proximate cause was held to be the accident, that is it was the direct and uninterrupted cause of death.

Similarly, it is suggested that if as a result of an accident, or in the context of the money policy an assault, a person suffered an embolism, due to lying inactive whilst recovering, the accident or assault would be the proximate cause of death and the policy would apply.

*Sole cause*

The use of the words "sole cause" can present another difficulty. Frequently, an accident or assault will cause an exacerbation of a pre-existing condition. That pre-existing condition may have been dormant — that is the injured person may not have been aware of it.

Certainly, if the accident or assault causes the disablement as a result of affecting the pre-existing condition, then it could not be said that it was the sole cause of it. Usually, the insurer will pay appropriate compensation, so far as it can be ascertained, for the injury itself, ignoring the effects of the pre-existing problem. It is frequently possible to assess when disability as a result of an accident or assault should have come to an end were it not for the other intervening cause.

It will have been seen that the personal accident extension makes reference to "compensation" (see above). This word has its ordinary meaning, that is a money payment reflecting the nature and extent of an injury received. It is frequently used, of course, as an alternative for the word "damages" which is a sum payable for injuries received as a result of a wrong or tort committed by another. Compensation has a wider meaning — that is the meaning used in a personal accident policy. It refers to an amount paid for an injury received.

There is usually an exclusion which reinforces the intention and meaning of the words requiring the injury to be independent of, and the sole cause of, death or disablement. A typical wording would be

> Compensation shall not be payable for death or disablement consequent upon the Insured or Director Partner or Employee of the Insured having any pre-existing physical or mental defect or infirmity of which he or the Insured became aware before the commencement of any Period of Insurance.

This wording does not exclude the payment of compensation to someone having a pre-existing physical defect; what it does is ensure that payment is not made for any disability or disablement arising as a result of it. Provided the injury can be separated from the pre-existing condition, then compensation can be paid for the injury alone. The other exception usually found in a personal accident policy or section, is one relating to death or disablement consequent upon pregnancy or childbirth.

## Definitions

As in personal accident policies, the personal accident extension of the money policy will frequently have a section defining certain words and phrases.

If the policy has not already referred to the age of the insured or partner, director or employee to whom the personal accident extension might apply, a clause under the heading "Definitions" will frequently do so. For example:

> For the purposes of this policy compensation will not be payable if the Insured or partner or Director or employee is aged less than 16 years or more than 70 years.

This same section of the extension, the definitions, usually clarifies what is meant by the "results" listed in the schedule.

The personal accident extension schedule varies from policy to policy, but typical "results" are as follows:

(a)  death,
(b)  total and permanent loss of all sight in one or both eyes,
(c)  loss of one or more hands or feet,
(d)  temporary total disablement.

It will be seen that the schedule clearly identifies the amount payable by way of compensation in any one event.


*Compensation*

Weekly compensation will only be paid in accordance with the limit shown on the schedule for "total disablement (temporary or permanent) from engaging in or attending to, usual employment or occupation".

Total disablement means exactly that; if the injured person is capable of any sort of work, for example supervisory duties, then the compensation will not be payable from the moment when that work is attempted. That does not mean, of course, that a person who does not normally carry out supervisory or clerical duties is required to attempt to do so as soon as he or she is physically capable. The wording refers specifically to "usual employment" and that applies to each individual.

Weekly compensation is limited to a period of either 52 or 104 weeks from the commencement of the result, that is from the commencement of the disablement and not necessarily from the moment of injury.

The compensation may also be restricted in the following ways:

(a)  The death or disablement must occur within one year of the injury being caused.
(b)  Only one of the death or permanent injury benefits will be paid and, of course, in each case it will be the higher sum if more than one is applicable. For example, if an unfortunate employee lost the sight of one eye and lost the use of one hand following an assault, only one payment would be made and if the benefits were different, that sum would, of course, be the higher one.

Finally, the maximum amount payable as the result of any assault is the amount payable on death. If then, an employee being totally disabled from attending his or her usual employment was paid weekly benefits and subsequently died, the amount of the weekly benefits would be deducted from the death benefit which then became payable.

## Conditions

Special conditions usually apply to the personal assault extension. The meaning of the words used is plain and it is sufficient to give examples of the usual conditions as follows.

> All certificates and information and evidence required by the Insurers shall be furnished at the expense of the Insured or any Claimant hereunder and shall be in such form and such nature as the Insurers shall prescribe.

Most insurers will require the completion of a claim or report form, and the forms used for claims under this particular extension usually contain a section which should be completed by the general practitioner or other medical attendant. Thereafter the claimant will be required to submit medical certificates by way of evidence of continued disability.

> The claimant shall, as often as required, submit to medical examination on behalf of the company at its own expense.

Medical examinations of this sort are usually required to ascertain whether or not sight is sufficiently damaged to be classed medically as permanent loss of all sight, or alternatively, to assess, independently, whether the loss of use of hands or feet should be considered, again medically, permanent loss of use.

There may also be occasions where it is necessary to obtain a medical opinion as to whether or not the person injured is still totally disabled from attending his or her usual employment.

> The Insurer in the case of death of the Insured or Director Partner or employee of the Insured shall be entitled to have a post-mortem examination at its own expense.

This condition enables the insurer to obtain what evidence may be available to ascertain whether or not death was independently and solely caused by bodily injury suffered by the assault.

The general conditions found in the money policy are similar to those in the theft policy and no additional comment is needed.

# CHAPTER 11

# All risks policies

## Introduction

Policies having in their descriptive title the words "all risks" are becoming more numerous. It has already been seen that the insurer needs to describe the risks against which the policy will provide protection carefully to ensure that, when providing cover, it can predict statistically the likely frequency and size of future claims. The insurer cannot, therefore, provide open ended policies giving protection against anything which may occur. To stay in business, the insurer needs to be precise and selective concerning the risks actually covered. The use of the words all risks, therefore, denotes a policy which, instead of listing the perils against which protection is provided, attempts instead to exclude events and contingencies against which protection is not provided. That is, in broad terms, if accidental damage occurs from a cause which is not excluded, then the policy operates.

The simplest form of all risks insurance cover is to be found as an extension to household policies.

If the items to be insured are particularly rare or valuable, it is sometimes necessary or recommended to have an all risks policy separate from the insured's household policy.

Whichever method of providing all risks cover is chosen, the policy wording and cover will be the same in principle, if not necessarily literally the same in every detail.

Even though household insurance policies can today be obtained which provide accidental damage cover, that cover will only apply to property within the house, or sometimes within the environs of the home. It is also usual for such a policy to limit the amount payable for items which can be described as "jewellery, furs, curios (or antiques) and works of art".

Some household policies may exclude any items in this category which individually exceed five per cent of the total sum insured. Other policies may limit the amount payable in respect of such items in any one loss to a maximum of one third of the total sum insured.

It will be appreciated, therefore, that the owner of valuables, antiques and works of art will not usually have sufficient protection from the household contents policy, whether that policy has accidental damage cover or not, but it should be noted that there will certainly be *no accidental damage cover when the property is removed from the home.*

Jewellery, antiques and other works of art are particularly susceptible to loss by theft. Thieves entering the home are more likely to take such items than others. It will also be appreciated that in the event of partial loss resulting from damage the cost of repairing the item in question will be substantially greater than would be the case with ordinary household effects. It is for this reason, therefore, that the household policy will restrict the amount payable.

The all risks policy is an ideal vehicle for providing insurance protection for such items.

A typical promise will read:

> If during any period of insurance, the property or any part thereof be lost or damaged by any accident or misfortune, the Insurer will by payment or at its option by reinstatement or repair, indemnify the Insured against such loss or damage. The liability of the Insurers during any one period of insurance shall not exceed in respect of each article, the sum insured set against such article in the Schedule.

The insurer requires to know precisely what is being insured.

The insured will have to list separately any item in order to have the protection of the insurance cover, and to describe it with enough accuracy to clearly identify it. Normally, a valuation will be provided by the insured to the insurer at the commencement of the policy cover as evidence of value *at that time.* It is very important to note that this is not an agreed value. All risks policies supported by valuations are not on those grounds agreed value policies. Those are an entirely different type of cover.

The insurer will calculate the premium due based upon the nature of each item to be insured and the value at risk.

### Miscellaneous valuables

It is normal to add an item to an all risks schedule headed "miscellaneous valuables". This item provides the same policy cover but for various smaller or less expensive items of jewellery, not individually valuable enough to be separately identified and listed, but which may at any one time be at risk.

It is normal to provide a single sum insured for all the miscellaneous valuables likely to be at risk at any one time, and a limit of value of any one item will also be included.

For example, the sum insured for the policy item described as "miscellaneous valuables" may be £2000 and the single article limit for each item perhaps £250.

It is interesting to note that the "miscellaneous valuables" item will frequently be subject to average.

As it is clearly the intention to provide insurance cover whilst any such item is away from home, the policy will not restrict cover to "whilst in the premises".

Cover is frequently provided "Anywhere in Great Britain and the Continent of Europe". Some policies may even give up to 60 days cover anywhere in the world.

Although the policy identifies the value of each item insured, it must be remembered that the all risks policy is still a policy of indemnity. The sum insured for each item is the maximum payable.

In the event of a specified item being lost, it may well be that it can be replaced, because of discounts available to insurers, at a cost less than the sum insured. If that is the case, then that is the measure of indemnity that the insurer can be called upon to pay. The insured cannot claim the sum insured, replace the item for a lower price and keep the difference.

Such difficulties may well arise not only as a result of discounts but also because the value of precious metals and stones does fluctuate, sometimes greatly. If the price of gold falls, and this reduces the cost of replacing a lost item, then the reduced price is the amount payable, even though the original sum insured may well have been established in relation to a professional valuation.

# Indemnity

## Sum insured

One reason for owning antiques and works of art is sometimes the capital appreciation which may be enjoyed thereby. The insured must always bear this in mind and take steps to increase the sum insured against each item appreciating in this way to ensure that in the event of a claim the sum insured is adequate.

It is usual to have the following additional exclusion in an all risks policy:

Loss or damage caused by wear and tear, depreciation or any gradually operating cause.

"Depreciation" has been considered above — that is, loss of value which takes place due to age. Wear and tear due to use of an article is inevitable and, therefore, excluded.

## Valued policy

In order to overcome some of these difficulties, it is sometimes possible to arrange a valued policy. Consideration of such policies was given earlier in the text; the policy is one where the value assigned to each article or item is agreed between the insurer and insured and that is the amount payable in the event of a total loss.

Such a policy is appropriate for works of art and antiques which may be difficult to value because similar items rarely become available for sale.

It should be remembered that by issuing such a policy, the insurer will still retain the right to repair or replace any item lost. The agreed value will not have an effect on the settlement of a claim for partial loss or damage. In that event, the cost of repair will be the measure of indemnity. Reference should be made to the fire insurance case, *Secock and Others v Thompson* (1949), where a partial loss by fire resulted in a proportion of the agreed value of the whole fire policy becoming payable.

## Pairs and sets clause

An area of difficulty frequently encountered in all risks policies is the measure of a loss when one of a set of items is damaged or lost — for example, one of a set of antique vases, or one of a pair of earrings.

In such an event, the insured might, not unreasonably, claim that the whole of the set had reduced in value by more than the proportion actually lost. If the insurer only intends to pay a due proportion in such an event, for example to pay 50% of the sum insured for a pair of earrings if one is lost or 33% of the sum insured for a matching trio of statuettes in the event of one being destroyed, then this will be made clear in the policy.

Historically, such a clause is called the "pairs and sets clause" and the following wording has been most frequently used:

> In the event of loss of or damage to any article forming part of a pair or set, the insurer shall not be liable for more than the value of the particular part or parts which may be lost or damaged without reference to any special value which such part or parts may have as forming a pair or set, but in any event, not exceeding a proportionate part of the sum insured in respect of the pair or set.

## Exclusions

One of the all risks exclusions has already been considered: it is also usual to exclude "Loss, damage or deterioration caused by moth or vermin" and "Loss or damage caused by any process of cleaning, repairing or restoring".

These are quite clear in their wording and are normally joined by the usual exclusions relating to "radioactivity" and "war risks" already considered in detail earlier in the text.

## Conditions

The conditions of the all risks policy are likely to be the same as policies already considered.

### Jewellery

When an all risks policy provides cover for jewellery it is common to add another condition. Jewellery is particularly susceptible to partial loss arising from the accidental detachment of precious stones and total loss resulting directly from the failure of fastenings.

Both types of loss can, of course, be reduced by regular maintenance and it is not unusual for the policy to make it a condition that the insured arranges regular maintenance, particularly for more valuable pieces.

A possible condition might read:

> It is a condition precedent to liability that the property insured shall at the expense of the Insured, be examined once every twelve months by a competent jeweller and written confirmation shall be obtained that the settings and fastenings are in order.

## Paintings

Some items normally insured on an all risks policy need special exclusions and conditions. Paintings may well have an exclusion relating to the effects of the atmosphere or light, as they are notoriously subject to fading.

## Musical instruments

Valuable musical instruments are particularly susceptible to damage or loss because they are frequently played and transported around the world. Policies providing cover for musical instruments will normally exclude losses arising from the breakage of strings, mechanical defects and loss or damage due to atmospheric or climatic conditions.

The policy will usually require that the instrument is carried in its specially designed case and travels with the owner or person responsible for it.

It was mentioned above that all risks cover is frequently an extension to the household contents policy.

There may be occasions when a loss takes place within the home, and amongst the items lost or damaged are one or more of those specified in the all risks extension, or separately insured by an all risks policy.

In the latter case, if the household contents policy excludes property more specifically insured, then each policy will act separately. Indeed, there would be no reason to include an allowance for the value of the specified all risks items within the household contents sum insured.

Otherwise, in the event of under insurance within the all risks policy, insurers are sometimes asked to contribute from the household contents sum insured to the extent that the specified items sums insured are insufficient (provided, of course, that the loss which has occurred is covered by the household contents policy).

As long as the household contents policy sum insured is sufficient to cover all the contents and the under insured proportion of the all risks sum insured, the contents insurers may sometimes be prepared to contribute.

If the wording of both policies is such that dual insurance has occurred (see earlier in the text) then the insurers will contribute following calculation of the amounts due by use of the independent liability method (again see earlier in the text) if one or other policy is subject to average. If there is no average clause, the ratio of sums insured would be appropriate.

# Business all risks policies

Policies denoted as all risks for businesses follow the same format, but in view of the extra risk and wider variety of property involved, the policies are, by necessity, more complex.

Policies which are described as "all risks property damage policies" are becoming more popular to replace the standard "fire and perils" and "engineering" type policies. Such policies frequently exclude theft losses and there is no provision in the schedule for sums insured relating to money.

It is not proposed to give any further consideration to this type of policy as this text is concerned with all risks covers which are more specific in their fields of application.

## "Package" policy

Most insurers provide, for small and medium sized businesses, "package" policies. The intention of these policies is to provide wide ranging cover for most, if not all, of the needs of the business concerned. Such policies are frequently aimed at a particular market, for example "shop policy" and "hotel policy". In addition to providing a combination of insurance covers available under separate policies, usually incorporating, of course, the protection available from fire, theft and money policies, it is possible also to include an all risks section.

The money section of the package policy follows invariably the format and wording of the money policy. The section relating to contents, however, frequently combines the protection afforded by fire and perils policies with that of the theft policy.

The operative clause or promise is typically as follows:

In the event of loss of or damage to the insured Contents at the Premises described in the Schedule caused by any of the Contingencies the Insurers will pay the Insured the value of the property at the time of the happening of its loss or the amount of such damage or at its option reinstate or replace such property or any part thereof.

The contingencies are then listed. Amongst those contingencies (ignoring for this purpose those normally listed in the fire and perils policies) would be the following:

Theft involving entry into or exit from the premises by forcible and violent means but excluding theft from any garden, yard or open space and any stable, garage, outbuilding or other building not communicating with the main premises unless specifically mentioned.

And:

Hold-up namely theft consequent upon and in connection with assault or violence, or threat thereof to the Insured or any employee of the Insured.

It will immediately be seen that the word "indemnity" is not used. However, the wording of the operative clause is sufficient to identify the extent of the insurer's responsibility in the event of a loss, but as was seen earlier in the text, indemnity is an overriding principle of insurance and the use of the word is not essential.

It will also have been noted that there is an absence of insurance cover for damage caused by thieves to the premises, which is given under a theft policy. This gap is rectified later in the contents section of such a policy under the heading "Extensions".

It will be remembered that "theft" has a specific meaning, as defined by the Theft Act 1968. The policy, therefore, restricts cover to losses involving forcible and violent entry or exit.

A typical wording for this part of the policy would be:

This Section extends to include — damage to the Premises falling to be borne by the Insured consequent upon Theft of the Contents involving forcible and violent entry into or exit from the premises or any attempt there at.

"... falling to be borne ..." was considered in the context of the theft policy. It means, of course, that the insured must be responsible for the repairs either as owner of the premises, or by being responsible for repairing such damage under the terms of the lease or other contract.

The contents section of this policy will also contain an "all other contents" part identical or similar to the section already considered. Average is included, but such policies frequently allow for seasonal increases in the sum insured, a practice mentioned earlier in the text.

This type of policy, that is the package policy, carries exceptions and conditions, but because of the combined nature of the cover, the exceptions for each individual section of the policy will usually be found within that section, and will be considered where relevant.

The package policy conditions are usually identical to those already considered in detail earlier in the text.

The all risks extension of such a package policy is, of course, subject to the terms and conditions of the policy. A typical wording would be:

The insurance by the Contents Section extends to include
Accidental loss or damage (not being loss or damage excluded by the Exceptions of this Section or Policy or excluded from any of the Contingencies of this Section). This extension does not cover:

a   The first £__ of each and every loss
b   Moveable property in the open
c   Property insured by the Glass Section of this Policy
d   Mechanical or electrical breakdown and/or derangement of machinery or equipment
e   Property damaged as a result of it undergoing any process
f   Cracking, fracturing, collapse or overheating of boilers, economisers, vessels, tubes or pipes, nipple leakage and/or the failure of welds to boilers
g   Loss of, or damage to computers and data processing equipment
h   Loss or damage caused by
    i    faulty or defective design materials or workmanship, inherent vice, latent defect, gradual deterioration, wear and tear or frost
    ii   subsidence, ground heave or land slip
    iii  normal settlement or bedding down of new structures
    iv   collapse or cracking of buildings
    v    theft or any attempt thereat, acts of fraud or dishonesty or any unexplained or inventory shortage
    vi   corrosion, rust, change in temperature, dampness, dryness, wet or dry rot, shrinkage, evaporation, loss of weight, contamination, change in colour, flavour, texture of finish, vermin, insects, marring or scratching

It will be seen that this extension has followed the basic format, ie it excludes those losses and contingencies that the insurer had not had in contemplation when assessing the risk and premium.

Property in the open (bearing in mind that this extension relates to contents) will inevitably suffer some loss or damage, if not by the action of thieves or vandals, then in time, by weathering.

Cover against damage to glass is, of course, available under a separate policy or section.

Mechanical or electrical breakdown is virtually inevitable sooner or later with machinery. Property undergoing a process is again at greater risk of damage (see below).

Damage to boilers and computers is the subject of other, very specialised types of insurance cover. The intention here is to avoid the overlapping of cover.

Items a - g relate, of course, to exclusion of property.

Item h relates to exclusions of contingencies. Whilst protection against subsidence damage is available under a household policy, it is normally not included in business policies.

Gradual deterioration, wear and tear and similar contingencies are of course inevitable, as will be frost damage if adequate protection is not provided.

The final exclusion by way of causes, that is corrosion, rust, etc relates to damage which will become inevitable if stock is not correctly stored. It is not the intention of the insurer to protect the insured against failure to organise the business correctly.

# CHAPTER 12

# Glass; goods in transit; fidelity guarantee

## Glass

A natural area for insurance cover in the nature of all risks is accidental glass breakage. Indeed, independent locally based companies offering only this type of cover existed some years ago.

The glass section of the "package" policy may have its own operative clause, for example:

> In the event of breakage of glass or sanitary ware described in the Schedule for which the Insured is responsible occurring at the premises the Insurers will reinstate such property or its option, pay to the Insured the cost of reinstatement. The Insurer shall not be liable to reinstate or pay for the reinstatement of such property exactly, but only to do so as nearly as circumstances permit and will pay the reasonable cost of boarding up incurred by such breakage.

It should be noted that emphasis is placed upon reinstatement. This is because the insurer frequently has the facility to instruct directly organisations which specialise in emergency boarding up and glass replacement. The advantage to the insurer is that such organisations allow a discount for accounts paid within certain time limits.

If the insurer does invoke this option, the protection of the second part of the clause is necessary, that is, that reinstatement need not be exactly as the glass was before, but only as close as circumstances permit. Were these words not in the clause, as has been seen already during consideration of reinstatement, the insurer may be liable to pay damages.

It should also be noted that the policy provides for replacement of the broken glass if the insured is responsible for it. The same principles of insurable interest apply here as in all other insurance matters. The insured must be either the owner of the premises or responsible for glass replacement under the terms of the lease.

## Exceptions

There are a few exceptions to the glass section. The first concerns breakages which would automatically be insured under other sections of the policy — for example, damage committed by malicious persons or thieves in the furtherance of theft. Even between sections of a policy, it is important to avoid duplication of insurance cover.

The other exception, so far as glass and sanitary ware are concerned, relates to pre-existing defects or damage occurring due to deterioration of frames or framework. This section may also include cover against accidental damage to signs. In that event, exceptions will apply concerning the need to maintain, repair or adjust the electrical signs falling within the definition.

## Goods in transit

Goods in transit insurance is generally dealt with by way of accidental or all risks cover, so protecting against damage to goods. It therefore falls naturally into the small business package policy. For example, a small business may wish to transport goods owned by it to customers or from suppliers, in its own transport. Alternatively, the company insured may wish to perform the same operation by post or by independent haulier.

Haulage contractors carrying property belonging to other people will need to cover their legal liability to the owners of the property carried; this can be done on an all risks basis. Such liability will usually arise by the contract conditions under which the haulage contractor trades. Usually, haulage contractors will belong to a trade association and will use that association's conditions — for example, the Road Hauliers'Association Conditions of Carriage under which the haulage contractor accepts liability up to a maximum value per tonne.

"Transit" has been held to mean the passage of goods from one place to another, and to include the time when the lorry in which they were being carried was temporarily parked (see *Sadler Brothers Company v Meredith* (1963)).

In *Sadler Brothers Company v Meredith*, the High Court held that "transit" was meant to have its ordinary meaning, that is the carriage of goods from one place to another. It was also held that the goods were still being carried and were still in transit even though the lorry in which they were being carried was temporarily parked. Roskill J said that an exhaustive definition of transit was impossible, but clearly the word related to the movement of the goods from one place to another and not the literal meaning of movement itself.

The duration of the transit insurance cover will normally be described by the policy, for example: "During loading and unloading and whilst temporarily housed during the course of such transit".

It should be noted that this cover includes loading and unloading which would not normally be considered part of the transit. Transit ceases when the goods are presented for delivery at the consignee's premises.

In *Crows Transport v Phoenix Assurance* (1965), the Court of Appeal held that goods were "temporarily housed" even though they had been left adjacent to an office during a lunch break whilst awaiting collection by hauliers.

A typical policy "promise" would be:

> In the event of any of the property being lost or damaged whilst in transit within Great Britain, Northern Ireland, the Republic of Ireland, the Isle of Man or the Channel Islands, the Insurers will by payment or at its option, by reinstatement or repair, indemnify the Insured against such loss or damage.

If the insured chooses to send goods by post or rail then, again, conditions of carriage will seek to restrict the liability of the carrier. Provided the insured has an adequate sum insured, this should cause no concern — only the insurer's recovery prospects will be affected.

When the insurance is being arranged, the sum insured should be carefully assessed and the basis of settlement agreed with the insurer. This is particularly important when finished goods are being delivered, as the insured's whole outlay may have been incurred and allowance for profit already calculated. In appropriate cases, the insurer may be prepared to pay claims based upon the insured's invoice value.

If the insured is exporting goods by sea, it will be necessary to ensure that the policy provides insurance cover until the goods are aboard ship.

In such circumstances the insured will probably contract with the customer to arrange carriage FOB (free on board) and will therefore need to ensure that the policy provides protection until the goods are in fact "over the ship's rail", at which time the marine policy will attach. (In fact, marine policies are available which include land transit, but are for special consideration.)

A typical extension required for export would be:

> In respect of any of the Property described in the Schedule despatched FOB, the insurers will pay for loss, destruction or damage occurring until delivered on board the export vessel including whilst remaining on quays, wharfs and/or in warehouses, whilst awaiting shipment, for a period not exceeding 60 days.

The exceptions are usually clearly worded and need no further explanation beyond the words commonly used.

The Company shall not be liable under this Section for:

1. Loss or damage due to vermin, insects, mildew, rust, depreciation, deterioration or changes brought about by natural causes.
2. Delay, loss of market or other consequential loss of any kind
3. Loss or damage by theft committed or connived at by an employee of the insured
4.   a   Money, securities or stamps
     b   Jewellery, watches, precious metals, precious stones or articles composed of any of them, furs or livestock unless specially mentioned as insured
5. Loss or damage caused by or attributable to default in packing or due to incorrect or insufficient addressing.

## Fidelity guarantee

The purpose of the fidelity guarantee section (and also of the fidelity guarantee policy available separately) is to protect an employer in the event of loss of money or property as a result of fraud or dishonesty by an employee or employees. The policy is one of indemnity and the basic principles, therefore, apply.

There must be insurable interest and in the event of a loss the insurer will, by way of subrogation rights, be able to seek recovery from the employee or employees concerned.

A typical promise would be:

The Insurers will indemnify the Insured in the event of loss of money or other property belonging to the Insured or for which he is responsible as a direct result of any act of fraud or dishonesty committed during the period of insurance by any of the Insured's employees and discovered

a   during the period of insurance, or
b   within two years thereafter or within two years after termination of the employment whichever happens first.

As already discussed, losses can occur by employees responsible for money removing funds over a period of time and disguising the fact by dishonest accounting practices, or by systematic removal of property (frequently stock) from the premises secretly and for their own gain.

The operative clause or promise sometimes requires that employees concerned must be identified; that is, it is not sufficient for the employer to note a loss of money or property, the employee or group of employees responsible must be identifiable.

Frequently, such losses are difficult to uncover and the policy allows the insured reasonable time in which to make the discovery. That is, the discovery needs to be made within two years of the losses occurring, or within two years of the termination of the responsible employee's employment, whichever is the earlier.

## Conditions

There are special conditions, relating to this section of the policy, but it should be noted that there is no requirement that the employee or employees concerned be prosecuted. Claims conditions require that the matter be reported to the police, but even if no prosecution ensues, or if a prosecution is brought and the employee is acquitted, the policy will still apply to losses which, "on the balance of probability", were perpetrated by that person or persons.

The special conditions normally require that any money held by the insured on behalf of the person or persons believed responsible, will be deducted from the amount of the loss. This will apply even if the insured hands over wages owed if that is done after the loss has been discovered.

The insurer will frequently attempt to make recovery. If the sum insured is not sufficient to meet the whole loss, then any monies recovered will first be paid to the insured to the extent of any uninsured loss, after taking into account costs incurred by the insurer.

With such a policy, it is of course essential that the insured maintain strict supervision over employees who may be in a position to act dishonestly. There is, therefore, a special condition pertaining to such matters which commences "it is a condition precedent to liability under this section that . . ." and then lists certain precautions which should be taken. It will be remembered that the use of those words allows the insurer to avoid policy liability in the event of a breach.

The insured is required to obtain written references for any employee who will be responsible for money, securities, stock or keeping accounts.

The insured may also be required to make sure that an employee different from the one receiving money is responsible for its storage, pending banking. Any employee who does so receive money, must bank it daily, or hand it to the insured or an employee specially authorised to receive that money.

Monthly statements of account must be sent to customers by an employee who is not responsible for collecting the money. If this were not the case, then an employee responsible for both sending out statements to customers and collecting the money, and who was tempted to indulge in dishonest practices, could retain cash or divert cheques and then ensure that the statements of account which would normally be produced and cause the customer to make an enquiry could be, instead, diverted. This would prevent the discovery of the dishonest act for a period of time.

The same considerations apply to ordering goods and authorising payment for them. The special conditions require these processes to be carried out by different employees acting independently.

In order to discover discrepancies quickly, it is usual to have a condition precedent to liability that monthly checks are made of bank statements, receipts, vouchers and documents relating to cash.

Finally, the special conditions require an annual independent stock check.

Other than the theft of money in small amounts over an extended period of time, the most usual fidelity guarantee loss will arise because employees have, over a period of time, removed stock.

This will only be possible if the insured's system of stock check is inadequate or has been allowed to fall into disuse in some way. An independent stock check should reveal both inadequacies in the stock control system and any fraudulent losses.

It may be that the insurer has agreed with the insured during the negotiations leading up to the issue of the policy that the systems of check are already adequate for the purposes of the insurance cover. In this case the insurer may issue a policy with a condition requiring the insured to maintain the system of check declared in the proposal, rather than issue a policy which lists, in the conditions, the detailed requirements mentioned above.

# CHAPTER 13

# Making a claim

## Introduction

It is the universal practice of United Kingdom insurers to attempt to handle claims sympathetically and by mutual co-operation. The fact remains however, that, as already explained, it is for the insured to show that a loss occurred to the property as a result of a cause against which the policy provides protection.

The insurer will consider the following:

(a) Did the loss occur from the premises as described? Difficulties can arise if the premises form only a portion of the building. Forcible and violent entry must be made through the perimeter of the premises as defined.

(b) Did the loss occur as defined in the operative clause? For example, was there forcible and violent entry to or from the premises in the case of the theft policy?

(c) Was the property stolen or damaged covered by the policy? Three aspects should be considered here. The property must be as defined in the schedule, it must be "pertaining to the business" and the insured must have an insurable interest.

(d) If the loss did occur as required by the operative clause, do any of the exclusions, exceptions or conditions apply?

(e) Were any additional or special warranties breached? It will be remembered that the theft policy in particular may have attached endorsements relating to specific protections by way of locks and alarms which must be complied with.

(f) Is the business as described in the policy? In particular, have there been any changes which will bring into effect the general condition concerning "Change of Interest"?

(g) How is the extent of the loss to be proved? Money losses are relatively easy to prove. What, though, is the value of stock or materials in trade, and machinery?

Machines which have been in use will be subject to wear and tear, and if replaced as new then the insured may be said to have received more than an indemnity if the policy does not have such a reinstatement clause which has agreed the basis of valuing the machinery for the purposes of a claim.

The cost of buying a secondhand machine may be considerably more than the written down value of the same equipment in the company accounts.

It has already been explained that the value of stock to a business will include the cost of transporting it to the premises as well as the cost of any work done to it. The cost of that additional work can be calculated by adding on labour costs, costs of direct power, supervision costs and administrative costs of the business directly concerned with the processing. Indeed if the insured is unable to reclaim VAT, then such tax paid will also be included in the loss calculation in relation to purchases made by the business.

In the course of proving insurable interest and value, the insured will inevitably produce invoices and Customs and Excise certificates where appropriate. There may be cases where the insured has not fully complied with the legal requirements. For example, the business may have avoided, by cash transactions, the payment of VAT or, as in the case of *Geismar v Sun Alliance and London Insurance Limited* (1977), imported property without declaring it to the Customs and Excise.

This case concerned a private individual, but would probably apply to a business also. The insured had imported jewellery into the United Kingdom but not declared it to the Customs. When it was stolen, the insurer refused to pay. The Queen's Bench Division agreed that there was no policy liability; the possession was tainted with illegality and it would be against public policy to allow the insured to recover. It should be remembered that the jewellery in question was intentionally concealed from the Customs; the court decision suggests that unintentional possession of such items would not defeat the policy.

(h) Do policy limits and average apply? Is there any possibility of recovery by the operation of the insurer's rights of subrogation? Enquiries carried out after a loss arising from theft, will of course, include liaison with the police. It should be understood that it is not the duty of the police to assist either the insured or the insurer to comply with their freely entered into contracts, and it would not be reasonable to expect them to provide information to either of the contracting parties to enable them to do so.

However, in the course of their enquiries, police officers may recover stolen or lost items, and it is then their duty to hold them until claimed (sometimes at the end of a court case if the items in question are evidence) by the person with the best title.

The Association of Chief Police Officers has issued guidelines for the supply of information to insurance companies. It is unnecessary to reproduce those guidelines in full but if they are followed police officers will do the following:

(i)    retain any letter from an insurance company, adjuster or claims assessor asking for information and/or requesting that their interest be noted;

(ii)   deal appropriately with any enquiry from an insurance company or adjuster or assessor where there is reasonable cause to believe that a claim may be fraudulent;

(iii)  file appropriately any correspondence from an insurance company confirming that settlement of a claim has been made and that title to property has passed to the insurer;

(iv)   if stolen property is recovered, the loser will be asked if any insurance claim has been settled and, if so, the property will be dealt with in accordance with the agreement between the "loser" and the insurer.

It should be emphasised that the guidelines are for advice only and individual circumstances may dictate different action.

These enquiries take some time. Depending upon the circumstances and the nature of the enquiries, it may be that the insurer does not make a payment with as much despatch as the insured feels appropriate. Should interest be paid? The existing authorities suggest that interest will not normally be payable unless it can be shown that the insurer wrongfully refused to pay, in which case interest will be awarded as damages (see *Webster v British Empire Mutual Life Assurance Company* (1880)).

Interest was awarded in special circumstances in the case of *Burts and*

*Harvey Limited and Alchemy Limited v Vulcan Boiler and General Insurance Company Limited* (1966). It appears that negotiations were protracted because the policy made it difficult to work out an appropriate indemnity. Lawton J said

> if insurance companies will issue policies which contain conditions which are inappropriate to a particular case, they can hardly say that it is the fault of the assured that it has been difficult to find out how much is due.

Interest was awarded. It should be emphasised, however, that this is a special case and as a rule, provided the insurer acts reasonably in the circumstances, interest will not be payable on the amount finally agreed as the loss sustained and paid in settlement of the claim.

# APPENDIX A

# *Security surveys*

The purpose of an insurance survey, whether carried out by a qualified and experienced surveyor or an experienced inspector from an insurance company, is to ascertain sufficient facts to enable the underwriter to assess properly the risk and calculate an appropriate premium.

Usually, the person carrying out the survey will have available the proposal form and will be able to check the information contained therein.

In the context of the theft and money policies, the surveyor will be particularly concerned with the nature and strength of the premises in question and the security precautions prevailing; that is, how easy or not it is to gain entry.

The surveyor will also be concerned with the locality and past claims experience.

All premises visited will be slightly different and it is not possible to provide "typical" examples of a survey. The surveys do, however, contain entries, other than name, address and a brief trade description, dealing with the following:

(a) Construction of the premises occupied by the proposer. In conjunction with this entry, there will usually be a plan showing the position of every door and window on each floor. The construction and protections and fastenings of each door and window will also be described.

(b) The location of the premises: are they in a main busy street or a quiet area? Can intruders approach unseen at any time, but particularly out of business hours?

(c) Where the proposer does not occupy the whole of the premises, the nature of any other occupants and businesses together with details of the protections available overall.

(d) Details of any persons who regularly sleep on the premises.

(e) A complete description of the contents and their value together with details of where each particular item will be stored.

Where items more susceptible to theft are kept (eg cigarettes), special details of the storage position of that stock with details of any special precautions taken will be required.

(f) A complete detailed and accurate description of any alarm already fitted.

(g) A complete and accurate description of any safe already installed.

(h) The nature and value of any cash or securities or other property normally kept in the safe.

(i) Details of previous losses with dates and amounts involved.

(j) Recommendations for additional protections.

(k) The surveyor's signature and the date.

The protections available, including a variety of locks, safes, high security doors and alarm systems which can be utilised, are extremely wide ranging.

Included here are diagrams of a rimlock and mortice lock, but even with these "everyday" locks there is a whole range of alternative levels of security and strengths.

Mortice locks considered suitable for protection are termed "deadlocks". An insurer will normally specify a "five lever" mortice deadlock as the minimum security accepted on a solid door. Such a lock operates by the key working a number of levers. The greater the number of levers, then the greater the number of possible keys which would be needed eventually to open the lock in question. The expression deadlock indicates that the bolt can only be moved backwards and forwards by means of the key. When the bolt is in its locked position, therefore, it would be necessary to break the door or frame in order to gain entry without a key.

Even here it is necessary to ensure that the door is thick enough to receive the lock in a "mortice" and still leave enough timber on either side to provide strength, or it may be necessary to strengthen the wood with metal plates secured by bolts passing through the door.

The "rim lock" is sometimes called a "night latch" and is a typical domestic or small retail shop door lock. It is of minimal value for security. A good hard kick at the door can usually force the two screws securing the keep from the door frame or even the latch from the door itself. Sometimes these locks have deadlock systems which mean the lock can not be forced by use of plastic inserted between the door and the frame (a simple method of opening doors if there is a space at the door edge, especially if the door is loose). These very brief comments on two locks indicate the complexity of the subject.

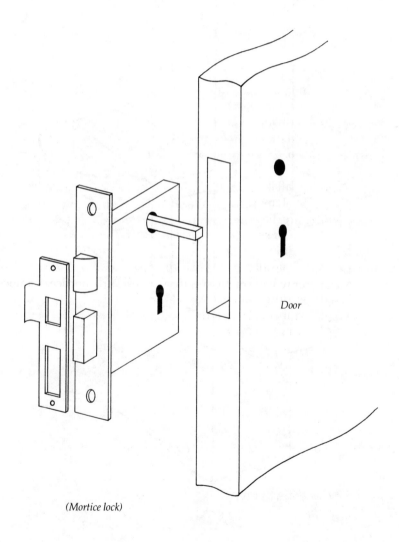

Door

(Mortice lock)

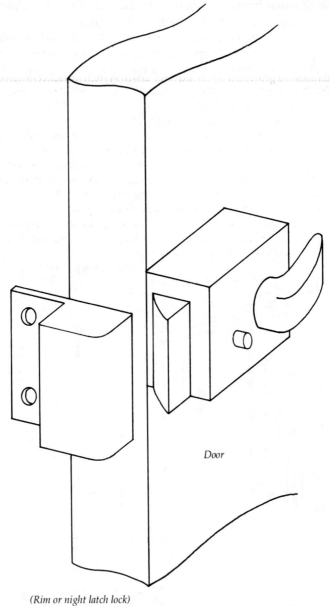

*Door*

*(Rim or night latch lock)*

# Alarm and protection condition

It is a condition precedent to the Insurers' liability for loss or damage under this policy that:

a.  Premises are protected by an intruder alarm system installed in accordance with the specification lodged with the insurers, and that a maintenance contract is maintained in force.
b.  The premises are not left attended unless
    1.  The intruder alarm system is tested and set in its entirety and where the system permits, has given such indication to signify that the external signalling system is connected and in full and effective operation.
    2.  All other security devices and protections existing at the date of this endorsement are in full and effective operation.
c.  The Insurer is notified immediately and in writing if:
    1.  The Insured is required to abate a nuisance under the code of practice on noise from audible Intruder alarms 1983 or received any written application from the police authority.
    2.  The Insured received any written application from the police authority regarding the withdrawal of their response to alarm calls.

# Association of British Insurers Statement of General Insurance Practice

The following Statement of normal insurance practice applies to general insurance of policyholders resident in the UK and insured in their private capacity only.

1. **Proposal forms**
   (a) The declaration at the foot of the proposal form should be restricted to completion according to the proposer's knowledge and belief.
   (b) Neither the proposal form nor the policy shall contain any provision converting the statements as to past or present fact in the proposal form into warranties. But insurers may require specific warranties about matters which are material to the risk.
   (c) If not included in the declaration, prominently displayed on the proposal form should be a statement.

      (i) drawing the attention of the proposer to the consequences of the failure to disclose all material facts, explained as those facts an insurer would regard as likely to influence the acceptance and assessment of the proposal;
      (ii) warning that if the proposer is in any doubt about facts considered material, he should disclose them.

   (d) Those matters which insurers have found generally to be material will be the subject of clear questions in proposal forms.
   (e) So far as is practicable, insurers will avoid asking questions which would require expert knowledge beyond that which the proposer

could reasonably be expected to possess or obtain or which would require a value judgement on the part of the proposer.

(f) Unless the prospectus or the proposal form contains full details of the standard cover offered, and whether or not it contains an outline of that cover, the proposal form shall include a prominent statement that a specimen copy of the policy form is available on request.

(g) Proposal forms shall contain a prominent warning that the proposer should keep a record (including copies of letters) of all information supplied to the insurer for the purpose of entering into the contract.

(h) The proposal form shall contain a prominent statement that a copy of the completed form:

   (i) is automatically provided for retention at the time of completion; or
   (ii) will be supplied as part of the insurer's normal practice; or
   (iii) will be supplied on request within a period of three months after its completion.

(i) An insurer shall not raise an issue under the proposal form, unless the policyholder is provided with a copy of the completed form.

## 2. Claims

(a) Under the conditions regarding notification of a claim, the policyholder shall not be asked to do more than report a claim and subsequent developments as soon as reasonably possible except in the case of legal processes and claims which a third party requires the policyholder to notify within a fixed time where immediate advice may be required.

(b) An insurer will not repudiate liability to indemnify a policyholder:

   (i) on grounds of non-disclosure of a material fact which a policyholder could not reasonably be expected to have disclosed;
   (ii) on grounds of misrepresentation unless it is a deliberate or negligent misrepresentation of a material fact;
   (iii) on grounds of a breach of warranty or condition where the circumstances of the loss are unconnected with the breach unless fraud is involved.
   Paragraph 2 (b) above does not apply to Marine and Aviation policies.

(c) Liability under the policy having been established and the amount payable by the insurer agreed, payment will be made without avoidable delay.

## 3. Renewal

(a) Renewal notices shall contain a warning about the duty of disclosure including the necessity to advise changes affecting the policy which have occurred since the policy inception or last renewal date, whichever was the later.

(b) Renewal notices shall contain a warning that the proposer should keep a record (including copies of letters) of all information supplied to the insurer for the purpose of renewal of the contract.

## 4. Commencement

Any changes to insurance documents will be made as and when they need to be reprinted, but the Statement will apply in the meantime.

## 5. Policy documents

Insurers will continue to develop clearer and more explicit proposal forms and policy documents whilst bearing in mind the legal nature of insurance contracts.

## 6. Disputes

The provisions of the Statement shall be taken into account in arbitration and any other referral procedures which may apply in the event of disputes between policyholders and insurers relating to matters dealt with in the Statement.

## 7. EEC

This Statement will need reconsideration when the Draft EEC Directive on Insurance Contract Law is adopted and implemented in the United Kingdom.

*Reproduced by permission of the Association of British Insurers.*

# APPENDIX C

# Sun Alliance Insurance Group shop insurance

## Proposal

Available only for shops in Great Britain, Northern Ireland, the Channel Islands and the Isle of Man.

Underwritten for the Group by Sun Alliance and London Insurance plc (incorporated in England).

**Please use block letters and tick boxes as appropriate.**

Full Name                                                          Tel. No.

Address of Shop                                                    Post Code

Business

Address for communications (if different from above)

**1  Property – Contents**

a) State full value of stock                    £ [          ]

b) State the declared value of General Contents  £ [          ]
   but exclude Specialist Equipment if to be
   insured separately

   Total sum to be insured                      £ [          ]

   See Prospectus for definition of 'declared value' and 'full value'

and, if included in a), of

tobacco and cigarettes      £ [          ]

wines and spirits           £ [          ]

photographic equipment  £ [          ]

blank or pre-recorded
video tapes                 £ [          ]

Please indicate if
a) Index Linking is not required                                        ☐

b) 'All Risks' cover is **not** required.                               ☐

**2  Business Interruption**
   Gross Profit Total sum to be insured (If more than £500,000)      £ [          ]

**3  Money**
   State (in multiples of £100) the maximum amount
   a) in the shop or in transit at any time **if more than £3,000**  £ [          ]

   b) in safe(s) overnight **if more than £1,000**                   £ [          ]

   Give details of make, model and age of each safe to be used

   [                                                                          ]

**Optional Cover – please select as required**

**4  Buildings**
   Full replacement cost of   a) Buildings                          £ [          ]

                              b) Tenants improvements               £ [          ]

                              Total declared value                  £ [          ]

   See Prospectus for definition of 'declared value'

   Please indicate if
   a) Index Linking is not required                                        ☐

   b) 'All Risks' cover is **not** required.                               ☐

**5  Deterioration of Stock**

| Make of cabinet/refrigerator | Model and h.p. | Number | Age | Full value of stock |
|---|---|---|---|---|
| a) | | | | £ |
| b) | | | | £ |

**6 Specialist Equipment** (see prospectus)

| Description including maker's number | Sum to be insured |
|---|---|
| a) | £ |
| b) | £ |

**7 Liability (Hairdressers only)**
a) Do you require cover for the treatment risk?                          Yes ☐  No ☐

b) If 'Yes', are any of the following provided:
sauna, massage, ear piercing or beauty treatment
(including ultra violet or similar equipment)?                            Yes ☐  No ☐

**8 Glass.**
i) Do you require cover for breakage of fixed glass and sanitaryware in the
private portion of the premises? (Only to be answered if you own or
otherwise occupy the premises as a private dwelling).                     Yes ☐  No ☐

ii) Is any of the Glass other than normal flat
annealed, toughened or laminated?                                         Yes ☐  No ☐

If 'Yes', please give description of glass, replacement value and situation.

**9 Transit** (to be answered only if more than
£1,000 Sum Insured required)
Please enter sum to be insured                                £

Number of own delivery vehicles if more than one

**10 Legal Expenses** (to be answered only if cover under this section is required).
a) State the total wageroll and salaries of staff in the following
categories in the last financial year
i) Directors, partners, managers and all non manual employees       £

ii) Manual employees including labour only sub-contractors           £

b) Does your dismissal procedure follow the guide laid down
in the 'Code of Practice 1' as prepared by ACAS?                          Yes ☐  No ☐

c) Provide details of any circumstances which could result in a dispute or give rise to any
payment under the Employment Disputes section; for example, employees subject to a
written or verbal warning, anticipated redundancies, recent or projected mergers
with another business.

e) Complete the following showing details of all
  i)   disputes arising out of employees' contracts of employment,
  ii)  prosecutions (excluding motor prosecutions) against the business, or any employee
       (arising out of his employment),
  iii) disputes with third parties relating to property owned by you or for which you are
       legally responsible, including any still pending, over the last three years.
  iv)  disputes with the Inland Revenue or Customs and Excise.

| Year of Incident | Brief Details | Outcome (if decided) including the amount of any settlement |
|---|---|---|
|  |  |  |

f) Provide
  i)   details and outcome of all non-employment contractual disputes over the last 3 years

|  |
|---|
|  |

  ii)  details of credit arrangements — e.g. credit level allowed without a credit check,
       maximum credit limit and period allowed.

|  |
|---|
|  |

11  Personal Accident

| Insured Persons Name | Date of Birth | Height | Weight | Number of Units |
|---|---|---|---|---|
|  |  |  |  |  |

12  Loss of Liquor Licence
  a) State the limits of indemnity required
    i)   On loss of Gross Profit (maximum indemnity period is 12 months)    £ [          ]

    ii)  On the reduction in value of the licensed premises    £ [          ]

  b) How long has the licence been in force?    [          ]

# GENERAL QUESTIONS

13  Do you wish to pay your premium by monthly instalments                     Yes ☐   No ☐

14  How long have you been in business

a) a these premises?

b) at any other premises?

15  have you previously insured for any of the covers to which this proposal
relates at these premises or elsewhere?                                        Yes ☐   No ☐

If 'Yes', give details including name of Insurers:

```



```

16  In respect of any of the risks to which this proposal relates and any business in which you
or any of your partners or directors are or having been engaged, whether at these premises
or elsewhere
a) have any accidents, losses or claims arisen in the last 5 years, whether insured or not   Yes ☐   No ☐

b) has any insurer declined a proposal, refused renewal, terminated
insurance or imposed special terms?                                        Yes ☐   No ☐

If 'Yes', give details

```



```

17  Have you, or any of your directors or partners been involved
in any other business in the last 5 years?                                     Yes ☐   No ☐
If 'Yes', please give details of each business including name, trade and dates

```



```

18  Have you, or any of your directors or partners ever been convicted
of or charged with (but not yet tried) a criminal offence other
than a motoring offence?                                                       Yes ☐   No ☐
If 'Yes', please give details

```



```

19  Do the shop premises communicate internally with a private
dwelling house occupied by you, your family or an employee?                    Yes ☐   No ☐

Declaration
(If any part of the Declaration does not apply please delete the appropriate clause and give
details in the space provided below)

I declare that
1   the premises are
    a) constructed of brick, stone or concrete and roofed with slate, tiles or concrete,
    b) not in an area subject to flooding,
    c) in a good state of repair and will be so maintained,
    d)in my/our sole occupation as saleshop in connection with the business or otherwise as
       offices or private dwellings only,

2   records of stocks, sales and purchases will be regularly maintained and balanced at least
    every 12 months,

3   all security devices will be in operation whenever the premises are closed for business.

4   All persons proposed for Personal Accident insurance are in good health, but have no physical
    or mental defect or infirmity and I will give immediate notice to the Company of any
    material change in the health of such persons.


Details of any amendments



I declare that these statements made by me or on my behalf are to the best of my
knowledge and belief true and complete and shall be incorporated in the contract between
me and the Sun Alliance and London Insurance plc.
I agree to accept a Policy in the Company's usual form for this class of insurance.

Signature                                                    Date



Signing this form does not bind you to complete the insurance.


We recommend that you should keep a record, including copies of letters and this
proposal form, of all information supplied to us for the purpose of entering into this
insurance contract.

Please let us know if you would like a copy of this proposal form sent to you.


*Reproduced by permission of Sun Alliance Group.*

## APPENDIX D

# *The business premises proposal form*

Name of Proposer in full                    Title: Mr/Mrs/Miss/Other
        Surname.
        Forenames.
        Business Name.

Postal Address.

Business Address (Premises from which trading takes place).

Nature of the Business.

How long have you occupied these premises?
Name and address of previous insurers if any.

When do you want insurance cover to commence?

Stock:
        Nature of the stock to be insured.
        (Please describe stock fully)

Value of Stock and other goods held in trust      £
Value of Machinery Trade & Office Furniture,
and All Other Contents.                            £
Money (weekly bankings)                            £

---

Premises:

Do you occupy the whole of the Premises?      YES/NO
If not describe the part occupied.

Are the Premises left unoccupied?             YES/NO
If so give details.

Do the Premises communicate with a
private dwelling house?                       YES/NO
Are the Premises built of brick, stone
or concrete and roofed with slates, tiles,
metal or concrete and in a good state of
repair?                                       YES/NO

---

Insurance History:

(For this business or any business owned by
or connected in any way with the Proposer
or any Director or Partner)
Has any Insurer ever declined Insurance?          YES/NO
Has any Insurer ever not invited renewal?         YES/NO
Has any Insurer cancelled or refused to
    renew Insurance?                              YES/NO
Has any Insurer imposed Special Conditions
    or increased premiums on renewal?            YES/NO
Have you suffered any losses by any of
    the causes to be insured within the last
    five years?                                   YES/NO
If yes, please give details:

Are Stock and Sales Records fully prepared
    and kept up to date?                          YES/NO

DECLARATION
I declare that the foregoing statements and particulars are true and complete and that this Proposal shall form the basis of the Contract with
(THE INSURER)


Signed:                                                        Date:

_____

# APPENDIX E

# *The theft policy and schedule*

The Insurers agree that if during any Period of Insurance
a) any of the Property while within the Premises shall be lost or damaged by Theft involving entry into or exit from the Premises by forcible and violent means or

b) there shall occur any damage to the Premises falling to be borne by the Insured consequent upon such Theft or any attempt thereat or

c) any of the Property shall be stolen from the Premises consequent upon and in connection with assault or violence or threat thereof to the Insured or any employee of the Insured

then the Insurers will by payment or at its option by reinstatement or repair indemnify the Insured against such loss or damage to the extent of and subject to the terms and conditions of this Policy.

**All other Contents**
The term All Other Contents includes
a) documents manuscripts and business books but only for the value of the materials as stationery with the cost of clerical labour expended in writing up and not for the value to the Insured of the information contained therein

b) computer systems records but only for the value of the materials together with the cost of clerical labour and computer time expended in reproducing such records (excluding any expense in connection with the production of information to be recorded therein) and not for the value to the Insured of the information contained therein

c) patterns models moulds plans designs but only for the value of the materials together with the cost of labour expended in reinstatement

d) so far as the same are not otherwise insured directors' employees' customers' and visitors' tools and other personal effects for an amount not exceeding £___ in respect of any one pedal cycle and £___ in respect of the tools and other personal effects of any one person

but to exclude
   i)   property referred to in the Exclusions

   ii)  wines spirits tobacco cigars and cigarettes except such property kept for entertainment purposes for an amount not exceeding £___

## Limits
The liability of the Insurers under this Policy during any Period of Insurance shall not exceed in respect of
   a) i)   any one item of the Property the Sum Insured stated in the Schedule

      ii)  damage to the Premises such sum as shall be sufficient to make good the damage

   b)   all loss or damage the Total Sum Insured

In the event of loss or damage covered by this Policy the Sums Insured shall forthwith stand reduced by the amount of such loss or damage unless the Insurers shall agree on payment of an additional premium to reinstate such Sums Insured

## Average
Each Item of Property is declared to be separately subject to Average that is to say if the property covered thereby shall at the time of any loss or damage be collectively of greater value than the sum insured thereon then the Insured shall be considered as being his own insurer for the difference and shall bear a ratable share of the loss or damage accordingly

## Exclusions
The Insurers shall not be liable in respect of
   1   Radioactive Contamination
       loss or destruction of or damage to any property whatsoever or any loss or expense whatsoever resulting or arising therefrom or any

consequential loss directly or indirectly caused by or contributed to by or arising from

i   ionising radiations or contamination by radioactivity from any nuclear fuel or from any nuclear waste from the combustion of nuclear fuel

ii  the radioactive toxic explosive or other hazardous properties of any explosive nuclear assembly or nuclear component thereof

2   War and Kindred Risks
any consequence of war invasion act of foreign enemy hostilities (whether war be declared or not) civil war rebellion revolution insurrection or military or usurped power riot or civil commotion

3   Fire and Explosion
loss or damage by fire or explosion however caused

4   Glass
damage to plate toughened laminated or stained glass or any decoration or lettering thereon

5   Connivance
loss or damage
a   by or with the connivance of any member of the Insured's household or any employee of the Insured or
b   occasioned by any person lawfully on the Premises

6   Property Specifically Excluded
loss of or damage to money securities tokens vouchers cheques coins stamps jewellery watches furs precious metals precious stones or articles composed of any of them tobacco cigars or cigarettes unless specially mentioned as insured hereunder

## Conditions

1   This Policy and Schedule shall be read together as one contract and any word or expression to which a specific meaning has attached in any part of the Policy or of the Schedule shall bear such meaning wherever it may appear

2   Reasonable Precautions
The Insured shall take all reasonable precautions for the safety of the Property including (a) the selection and supervision of employees (b) the securing of all doors and windows and other means of entrance

3    Change of Risk and Values
     No claim shall be recoverable hereunder (a) if any material change
     shall be made in the Premises or in the conditions of the risk as
     existing at the time of the acceptance or (b) if the intrinsic value of
     the contents of the Premises be at any time materially increased
     unless in such cases the written consent of the Insurers has been
     obtained

4    Change of Interest
     The interest of the Insured under this Policy shall not be assignable
     except with the written consent of the Insurers

5    Claims — Action by Insured
     Immediately upon having knowledge of any event giving rise or
     likely to give rise to a claim under this Policy the Insured shall:
     a)   give notice to the police and render all reasonable assistance in
          causing the discovery and punishment of any guilty person and
          in tracing and recovering the Property
     b)   give notice thereof to the Insurers in writing and within thirty
          days thereafter or such further time as the Insurers may allow
          deliver to the Insurers a claim in writing and supply all such
          detailed proofs and particulars as may be reasonably required
     In no case shall the Insurers be liable for any loss or damage not
     notified to the Insurers within thirty days of the event

6    Control of Claims
     In the event of a claim being made against the Insurers under this
     Policy
     a)   the Insurers may at any time at its own expense use all legal
          means in the name of the Insured for recovery of any of the
          Property lost and the Insured shall give all reasonable assistance
          for that purpose
     b)   the Insurers shall be entitled to any Property for the loss of which
          a claim is paid hereunder and the Insured shall execute all such
          assignments and assurances of such Property as may be reason-
          ably required but the Insured shall not be entitled to abandon
          any Property to the Insurers

7    Other Insurances
     If at the time of any loss or damage there be any other insurance
     effected by or on behalf of the Insured covering any of the Property

the liability of the Insurers hereunder shall be limited to its ratable proportion of such loss or damage

If any such other insurance is expressed to cover any of the Property hereby insured but is subject to any provision whereby it is excluded from ranking concurrently with this Policy either in whole or in part or from contributing ratably to the loss or damage the liability of the Insurers hereunder shall be limited to such proportion of the loss or damage as the sum hereby insured bears to the value of the Property

8    Cancellation

The Insurers may cancel this Policy by sending seven days notice by registered letter to the Insured at his last known address and in such event the Insured shall become entitled to the return of a proportionate part of the premium corresponding to the unexpired Period of Insurance

9    Arbitration

If any difference shall arise as to the amount to be paid under this Policy (liability being otherwise admitted) such difference shall be referred to an Arbitrator to be appointed by the parties in accordance with the Statutory provisions in that behalf for the time being in force Where any difference is by this condition to be referred to Arbitration the making of an award shall be a condition precedent to any right of action against the Insurers

10    The due observance and fulfilment of the terms and conditions of this Policy in so far as they relate to anything to be done or complied with by the Insured and the truth of the statements in the Proposal made by the Insured shall be Conditions Precedent to any liability of the Insurers to make any payment under this Policy

# Theft Policy Schedule

The insured.

Name
Address

Postcode

___

The Business.

and no other for the purpose of this Indemnity

Period of Insurance.
 a) From
    To
 b) Any subsequent period for which the Insured shall pay
    and the Insurers shall agree to accept a renewal premium

___

First Premium          £
Renewal Premium        £

___

The Premises.
exclusive of any garden yard or open space and any building not
communicating with the main Premises unless specially mentioned

It is warranted that the building of which the Premises form a part is
otherwise normally inhabited as a private residence by the Insured or by
an employee of the Insured charged with the care of the Premises.

___

The Property pertaining to the Business.

A) Stock and materials in trade the property of the Insured
   and goods in trust or on commission for which the
   Insured is responsible
Sum Insured            £

B) Machinery plant trade and office furniture fixtures fittings and All Other Contents the property of the Insured or for which the Insured is responsible excluding stock and materials in trade goods in trust or on commission and property more specifically insured

Sum insured                    £

Total Sum Insured        £

# APPENDIX F

# The money policy and schedule

The Insurers agree that during any period of Insurance in the event of

a) Loss of Money
b) Loss of or damage to
   i) Safe or Strongroom
   ii) Case bag or waistcoat when such is used for the carriage of money

Directly associated with any theft or attempted theft therefrom except in so far as this cost is otherwise insured

c) Loss or damage to clothing and personal effects being sustained by the Insured or any Director Partner or Employee of the Insured as a result of an assault by a person or persons attempting to steal money

Occurring in the Situations described in the Schedule the Insurers will indemnify the Insured against such loss or damage to the extent of and subject to the terms and conditions of the Policy

**Territorial Limits**
Within Great Britain Northern Ireland the Republic of Ireland the Channel Islands and the Isle of Man

**Definitions**
Money
   Cash Bank and Currency Notes Girocheques Cheques Postal and Money Orders Crossed Bankers' Drafts Premium Bonds Savings Certificates Stamps Unexpired Units in Franking Machines National Insurance Stamps National Savings and Holidays with Pay Stamps Luncheon Vouchers Credit Card Sales Vouchers Trading Stamps

Gift Tokens Consumer Redemption Vouchers and V.A.T. Purchase Invoices

Business Hours
The Period during which the Insured's Premises or Sites of Contract are actually occupied for business purposes and during which the Insured or any Director Partner or Employee of the Insured entrusted with Money is in the Premises or at Sites of Contract

---

# Money Policy Schedule

The Insured.
Name
Address

Postcode

---

The Business.
and no other for the purpose of this Insurance

---

Period of Indemnity.
a) From
To
b) Any subsequent period for which the Insured shall pay and the Insurers shall agree to accept a renewal premium

---

First Premium          £
Renewal Premium        £

---

The liability of the Insurers shall not exceed in respect of

A. Any single loss of Bank notes currency notes uncrossed bankers' drafts uncrossed postal orders uncrossed money orders uncrossed cheques

   i During business hours anywhere within the
     Territorial Limits                                    £
  ii Out of business hours in the Premises not
     secured in a locked safe or strongroom         £
 iii Out of business hours in the Premises
     secured in a locked safe or strongroom         £
  iv In the residences of the Insured or
     Director Partner or Employee of the Insured   £
   v Any other single loss of Money              £

B Any single loss of crossed cheques crossed
   giro cheques crossed bankers' drafts crossed money
   orders National Savings Certificates Premium Bonds
   credit and sales vouchers and V.A.T. invoices   £
                                        (eg £250,000)

C Safe or Strongroom
   Case bag or waistcoat used for
   the carriage of Money                 Cost of repair
                             or replacement

   Clothing and personal effects of
   the Insured or Director Partner or
   Employee of the Insured                 £
                                   (eg £100)

---

## Personal Accident Scale of Compensation

   1 Death                                  £
   2 Total and permanent loss of sight
     in one or both eyes                £
   3 Loss of one or both hands or feet       £
   4 Total disablement (per week)          £

# Personal Accident Extension

The Insurers agree that if as a result of an attempt to steal
   a) Money Insured by this Policy
   b) Stock in trade belonging to the Insured from the Premises
       while the Premises are open for business
the Insured or Director Partner or Employee of the Insured shall suffer
bodily injury and which injury shall independently of any other cause be
the sole cause of death or disablement the Insurer will pay to the Insured
the compensation specified in the Schedule for any of the results specified

## Definitions and Limitations
   1   For the purposes of this Policy Compensation will not be payable if
       the Insured or Director Partner or Employee is aged less than sixteen
       or more than seventy years of age
   2   Results
       i    Death
       ii   Total and permanent loss of sight in one or both eyes
       iii  Loss of one or both hands or feet
       iv   Total disablement from attending to or engaging in usual em-
            ployment or occupation

## Compensation
Compensation for Result iv shall be payable for a period not exceeding 52
weeks from the commencement of the Result
Compensation shall not be payable for
   i    any of the results unless such result occurs within one year of
        sustaining the injury
   ii   more than one of the Results

## Exclusions
Compensation shall not be payable for death or disablement consequent
upon the Insured or Director Partner or Employee of the Insured having
any pre-existing physical or mental defect or infirmity of which he or the
Insured became aware before the commencement of any Period of Insurance

## Special Conditions
   1   All certificates and information and evidence required by the
       Insurers shall be furnished at the expense of the Insured or any

claimant hereunder and shall be in such form as the Insurers shall prescribe

2    The Claimant shall as often as required submit to medical examination on behalf of the Insurers at its own expense

3    The Insurers in the case of death of the Insured or Director Partner or Employee of the Insured shall be entitled to have a post-mortem examination at its own request

**Exclusions**

The Insurers shall not be liable in respect of

1    Radioactive contamination

loss or destruction of or damage to any property whatsoever or any loss or expense whatsoever resulting or arising therefrom or any consequential loss directly or indirectly caused by or contributed to by or arising from

i    ionising radiations or contamination by radioactivity from any nuclear fuel or from any nuclear waste from the combustion of nuclear fuel

ii    the radioactive toxic explosive or other hazardous properties of any explosive nuclear assembly or nuclear component thereof

2    War and Kindred Risks

any consequence of war invasion act of foreign enemy hostilities (whether war be declared or not) civil war rebellion revolution insurrection or military or usurped power riot or civil commotion

3    Dishonesty of Employees

any loss arising from fraud or dishonesty of any Employee of the Insured

a)    unless discovered within seven days of its occurrence

b)    covered by a policy of Fidelity Guarantee insurance

4    Errors

shortages due to error or omission

5    Unattended Vehicles

loss from any unattended vehicle

## APPENDIX G

# Sun Alliance Insurance Group all risks policy

PLEASE READ THIS POLICY (AND THE SCHEDULE WHICH FORMS AN INTEGRAL PART OF THE POLICY) TO ENSURE THAT IT MEETS YOUR REQUIREMENTS

Sun Alliance and London Insurance plc (incorporated in England and herein called the Company) and the Insured agree that

This Policy the Schedule (including any Schedule issued in substitution) and any Memoranda shall be considered one document and any word or expression to which a specific meaning has been attached shall bear such meaning wherever it appears

The Proposal or any information supplied by the Insured shall be incorporated in the contract

The Company will provide the insurance described in this Policy subject to the terms and conditions for the Period of Insurance shown in the Schedule and any subsequent period for which the Insured shall pay and the Company shall agree to accept the premium

Provided that this Policy shall not be in force unless it has been initialled by an authorised official of the Company

Chief General Manager

Initialled

# General Conditions

This Policy shall be voidable in the event of misrepresentation misdescription or non-disclosure in any material particular

Observance of the terms of this Policy relating to anything to be done or complied with by the Insured is a condition precedent to any liability of the Company

The Insured at his own expense shall

A) take all reasonable precautions to prevent or diminish loss destruction or damage
B) exercise care in the selection and supervision of employees

The insurance by this Policy shall cease if
A) the Business is wound up or carried on by a liquidator or receiver or permanently discontinued or
B) the Insured's interest ceases otherwise than by death or
C) any alteration be made either in the Business or in the Premises or property therein or any other circumstances whereby the risk is increased
at any time after the commencement of this insurance unless the Company shall have been notified in writing and has agreed in writing to the continuation of the insurance

If any part of the Premium or Renewal Premium is based on estimates provided by the Insured the Insured shall keep an accurate record containing all relevant particulars and shall allow the Company to inspect such record The Insured shall within one month after the expiry of each Period of Insurance provide such information as the Company may require The Premium shall then be adjusted and the difference paid by or allowed to the Insured

The Company or the Insured may cancel this Policy by giving 30 days notice in writing to the other party at its last known address If the Company gives such notice the Insured shall become entitled to a proportionate return of premium If the Insured gives such notice the Insured shall be entitled only to a return premium in accordance with the Company's usual short period scale provided that no claim has been made in the then current Period of Insurance

# Claims Conditions

If any claim shall be in any respect fraudulent or if any fraudulent means or devices are used by the Insured or anyone acting on behalf of the Insured to obtain any benefit under this Policy or if any loss destruction or damage is occasioned by the wilful act or with the connivance of the Insured all benefit under this Policy shall be forfeited

On the discovery of any event which may give rise to a claim under this Policy the Insured shall

A) notify the Company in writing forthwith
B) give immediate notice to the police authority in respect of loss destruction or damage caused by malicious persons or by thieves and take all reasonable steps to discover any guilty person and recover the property lost
C) carry out and permit to be carried out any action which may be reasonably practicable to avoid or diminish the loss destruction or damage and to prevent further loss destruction or damage
D) within 30 days after the event or such further time as the Company may allow at his own expense delivery to the Company
   1) full information in writing of the claim
   2) details of any other insurance relating to the claim
   3) all such business books documents proofs information explanation and other evidence as may be reasonably required all of which information and details may be produced by the Insured's professional accountants or auditors who are regularly acting as such their report being prima facie evidence of such information and details
   4) if demanded a statutory declaration of the truth of the claim and of any matter connected with it

## Applicable only to Section 1 Money

The Insured shall at the Company's request and expense do and concur in doing and permit to be done all such acts and things as may be necessary or reasonably required by the Company for the purpose of enforcing any rights and remedies or of obtaining relief or indemnity from other parties to which the Company shall be or would become entitled or subrogated upon the Company paying for or making good any loss under this Policy whether such acts and things shall be or become necessary or required before or after the Company indemnifies the Insured

If any difference shall arise as to the amount to be paid under this Policy (liability being otherwise admitted) such difference shall be referred to an arbitrator to be appointed by the parties in accordance with the statutory provisions in that behalf for the time being in force Where any difference is by this condition to be referred to arbitration the making of an award shall be a condition precedent to any right of action against the Company

# Crime Insurance — Theft

If during the Period of Insurance the property insured described in the Schedule or any part of such property is lost destroyed or damaged by Theft while within that part of the Premises occupied by the Insured for the purpose of the Business the Company will pay to the Insured the value of the property at the time of the happening of its loss or destruction or the amount of such damage or at its option reinstate or replace such property or any part of such property

the Company will in addition indemnify the Insured in respect of
1) damage for which the Insured is responsible to the buildings at the Premises resulting from such Theft provided that such damage is not otherwise insured
2) reasonable expenses not exceeding £500 incurred in necessarily replacing locks consequent upon Theft of keys to such building or safes or strongrooms therein from such building or from the residence of any of the authorised keyholding directors partners or employees of the Insured

Provided that
1) the liability of the Company shall in no case exceed in respect of each item the sum expressed in the Schedule to be insured thereon or in the whole the Total Sum insured hereby
2) if the Company elect or become bound to reinstate or replace any property the Insured shall at his own expense produce and give to the Company all such plans documents books and information as the Company may reasonably require The Company shall not be bound to reinstate exactly or completely but only as circumstances permit and in reasonably sufficient manner and shall not in any case be bound to expend in respect of any of the items insured more than the sum insured thereon

**Definitions and Interpretations**

Theft shall mean actual or attempted theft from a building other than an outbuilding not communicating with the main building unless specifically mentioned in the Schedule or by Memorandum
A) involving entry to or exit from a building by forcible and violent means
B) following actual or threatened assault or violence

Money shall mean
Cash bank notes currency notes cheques bankers' drafts postal orders money orders current postage stamps and revenue stamps National Insurance Stamps National Savings stamps and certificates holiday savings stamps luncheon vouchers credit company sales vouchers VAT purchase invoices Premium Bonds bills of exchange giro cheques and draft gift tokens trading stamps unused units in franking machines consumer redemption vouchers and credit cards

General Contents shall mean
A) Machinery plant fixtures fittings and trade utensils
B) Documents manuscripts business books and computer systems records but only for the value of the materials as stationery together with the cost of clerical labour and computer time expended in writing up such documents manuscripts and business books or reproducing such computer systems records (excluding any expense in connection with the production of information to be recorded therein) and not for the value to the Insured of the information they contain
C) Patterns models moulds plans and designs
D) Tenants' improvements alterations and decorations for which the Insured is responsible
E) So far as they are not otherwise insured directors' partners' and employees' personal effects (including clothing pedal cycles tools instruments and the like but excluding articles partly or wholly of precious metal jewellery watches furs contact lenses portable electronic entertainment equipment cameras money and securities of any description) for an amount not exceeding £250 per person unless otherwise stated in this Policy
F) Wines spirits cigarettes and tobacco held for entertainment purposes not exceeding £250 in total
all belongings to the Insured or held by the Insured in trust or on commission for which the Insured is responsible
General Contents shall not include landlords' fixtures and fittings stock and materials in trade work in progress or any other property more specifically insured

Stock and Materials in trade shall mean stock and materials in trade and work in progress belonging to the Insured or held by the Insured in trust or on commission for which the Insured is responsible but excluding property more specifically insured

**Exclusions**

The Company shall not be liable for

1   loss or destruction of or damage to
    A) glass if more specifically insured
    B) Money

2   property in the open unless specifically mentioned in the Schedule or by Memorandum

3   loss destruction or damage by or in consequence of
    A) Fire
    B) Exlosion unless caused by the use of explosives in the course of Theft when the liability of the Company shall not exceed £25,000 or the Total Sum Insured whichever is the less

**4** consequential loss or damage of any kind or description

**5** loss or destruction of or damage to property which at the time of the
happening of such loss destruction or damage is insured by or would but for
the existence of this Policy be insured by any marine policy or policies except
in respect of any excess beyond the amount which would have been payable
under the marine policy or policies had this insurance not been effected

**6** loss destruction or damage
A) directly or indirectly occasioned by or happening through or in
consequence of
1) war invasion act of foreign enemy hostilities (whether war be declared
or not) civil war rebellion revolution insurrection or military or usurped
power
2) riot or civil commotion in Northern Ireland
B) to any property whatsoever or any loss or expense whatsoever resulting or
arising therefrom or any consequential loss directly or indirectly caused by
or contributed to by or arising from
1) ionising radiations or contamination by radioactivity from any nuclear
fuel or from any nuclear waste from the combustion of nuclear fuel
2) the radioactive toxic explosive or other hazardous properties of any
explosive nuclear assembly or nuclear component thereof

C) directly occasioned by pressure waves caused by aircraft and other aerial
devices travelling at sonic or supersonic speeds

**Special Conditions and Extensions**

**1** Security Precautions
It is a condition precedent to the Company's liability for loss or damage that

A) in respect of any Intruder Alarm System installed at the Premises

1) a maintenance contract is maintained in force during the currency of the
Policy with the installing contractor or such other contractor as is agreed
in writing by the Company
2) the Business Premises are not left unattended unless
A) the Intruder Alarm System is tested and set in its entirety and where
the equipment permits any Central Station to which the Intruder
Alarm System is connected has acknowledged the setting signal and
B) as far as the Insured or his representative is aware the Intruder
Alarm System is in full and efficient working order
3) the agreement of the Company is obtained in writing before replacing
extending or otherwise altering the Intruder Alarm System
4) the Company is notified immediately and in writing if
A) the Insured receive written notification from a police authority that

they may be withdrawing response to alarm calls or
B) the Insured is required to abate a nuisance under the Code of
Practice on Noise from Audible Intruder Alarms 1983 or by the Force
policy issued by the Chief Constable
B) whenever the Premises are left unattended
1) all locks bolts and other protective devices are in full operation
2) All keys (including those relating to any part of the Intruder Alarm
System) are
A) removed from the Business Premises or
B) placed within a locked safe or strongroom the keys to which are
themselves removed from the Business Premises

Interpretation
Intruder Alarm System shall be deemed to include all lines and equipment used
to transmit the signals to and from the Premises

2  Underinsurance Condition (Average)

Unless otherwise stated the Sum Insured by each item of the Policy is
declared to be separately subject to the Underinsurance Condition namely

Whenever a Sum Insured is declared to be subject to the Underinsurance
Condition if the property covered thereby shall at the commencement of any
loss destruction or damage hereby insured against be collectively of greater
value than such Sums Insured then the Insured shall be considered as being
his own insurer for the difference and shall bear a ratable share of the loss
accordingly

3  Index Linking
If shown in the Schedule as Applicable the Company will adjust the Sums
Insured in line with the Department of Trade and Industry Monthly Producer
Price Index — Output or an alternative index selected by the Company
No responsibility shall attach to the Company if publication of any index is
delayed but at the Company's discretion an estimated figure may be used
The Renewal premium will be based on the adjusted Sums Insured

4  Automatic Reinstatement of Loss
On the first occasion of loss damage or destruction in any one Period of
Insurance in the absence of written notice by the Company or by the Insured
within thirty days to the contrary the Sums Insured by this Policy will not be
reduced by the amount of the loss subject to the Insured paying the
appropriate additional premium on the amount of the loss

5  Contract Price
It is hereby agreed and declared that in respect only of goods sold but not
delivered for which the Insured is responsible and with regard to which under
the conditions of the sale the sale contract is cancelled by reason of any loss
damage or destruction hereby insured against either wholly or to the extent of

the loss destruction or damage the liability of the Company shall be based on the contract price and for the purpose of the Underinsurance Condition the value of all goods to which this clause would in the event of loss damage or destruction be applicable shall be ascertained on the same basis

**6 Designation of Property**
Where necessary the item heading under which any property is insured shall be determined by the designation under which such property has been entered in the Insured's books

**7 Motor Vehicles**
Motor vehicles motor chassis and their contents are included in this insurance to the extent that such property is not otherwise insured

**8 Professional fees**
The insurance by each item on Buildings and General Contents includes an amount in respect of Architects' Surveyors' Consulting Engineers' Legal and other Professional Fees necessarily incurred in the reinstatement of the property insured consequent upon its loss damage or destruction but not for preparing any claim it being understood that the amount payable for each loss destruction or damage and fees shall not exceed in the aggregate the Sum Insured by each item

**9 Reinstatement Conditions**

It is hereby agreed that in the event of the property insured under the General Contents item of this policy (other than motor vehicles and motor chassis directors' and employees' personal effects if insured hereby) being lost destroyed or damaged the basis upon which the amount payable under each of the said items of the policy is to be calculated shall be the reinstatement of the property destroyed or damaged subject to the following special provisions and subject also to the terms and conditions of the policy except in so far as the same may be varied hereby

For the purposes of the insurance under this extension reinstatement shall mean
The carrying out of the aftermentioned work namely
A) Where property is lost or destroyed its replacement by similar property in a condition equal to but not better nor more extensive than its condition when new
B) Where property is damaged the repair of the damage and the restoration of the damaged portion of the property to a condition substantially the same as but not better nor more extensive than its condition when new

Special Provisions

1   The work of reinstatement (which may be carried out upon another site and in any manner suitable to the requirements of the Insured subject to the

liability of the Company not being thereby increased) must be commenced
and carried out with reasonable despatch otherwise no payment beyond
the amount which would have been payable under the Policy if this
extension had not been incorporated therein shall be made
2  When any property insured under this extension is damaged or destroyed
in part only the liability of the Company shall not exceed the sum
representing the cost which the Company could have been called upon to
pay for reinstatement if such property had been wholly destroyed
3  No payment beyond the amount which would have been payable under the
Policy if this extension had not been incorporated therein shall be made
until the cost of reinstatement shall have been actually incurred
4  Each item insured under this extension is declared to be separately subject
to the following Underinsurance Condition namely
If at the time of reinstatement the sum representing eighty-five per cent
of the cost which would have been incurred in reinstatement if the whole
of the property covered by such item has been destroyed exceeds the
Sum Insured thereon at the commencement of any loss destruction or
damage hereby insured against then the Insured shall be considered as
being his own insurer for the difference between the Sum Insured and
the sum representing the cost of reinstatement of the whole of the
property and shall bear a ratable proportion of the loss accordingly
5  No payment beyond the amount which would have been payable under the
Policy if this extension had not been incorporated therein shall be made if
at the time of any loss destruction or damage to any property insured
hereunder such property shall be covered by any other insurance effected
by or on behalf of the Insured which is not upon the identical basis of
reinstatement set forth herein
6  Where by reason of any of the above Special Provisions no payment is to
be made beyond the amount which would have been payable under the
Policy if this extension had not been incorporated therein the rights and
liabilities of the Company and the Insured in respect of the loss destruction
or damage shall be subject to the terms and conditions of the Policy
including any Underinsurance Condition therein as if this extension had not
been incorporated therein

**10** Temporary Removal
Subject to the aftermentioned provisions the following property insured by this
Policy is covered while temporarily removed to any premises in Great Britain
Northern Ireland the Channel Islands the Isle of Man or the Republic of Ireland
A) deeds and other documents (including stamps thereon) manuscripts plans
and writing of every description books (written and printed) and computer
systems records on the basis provided under the General Contents clause
for an amount not exceeding 10% of the value of such property
B) other property for cleaning renovation repair or other similar purposes for
an amount not exceeding 10% of the Sum Insured by the item after
deducting therefrom the value of any building (exclusive of fixtures and
fittings) stock or materials in trade insured thereby

The amount recoverable under this extension in respect of each item of the Policy shall not exceed the aforementioned limits and in respect of the property insured under B) shall exclude
1) stock or materials in trade insured thereby
2) property more specifically insured
3) motor vehicles and motor chassis licensed for normal road use
4) property held by the Insured in trust other than machinery and plant

**11** Waiver of Subrogation Rights
In the event of a claim arising under this Policy the Company agrees to waive any rights remedies or relief to which they might become subrogated against
A) any company being Parent of or Subsidiary to the Insured as defined in Section 154 of the Companies Act 1948 or Section 148 of the Companies Act 1960 (Northern Ireland)
B) any company which is a Subsidiary of a Parent company of which the Insured are themselves a Subsidiary in each case within the meaning of Section 154 of the Companies Act 1948 or Section 148 of the Companies Act 1960 (Northern Ireland)

# Money Insurance

### Section 1 Money

The Company will indemnify the Insured up to the Limit of Liability for any loss of or damage to the Money and property described in Items 1 to 5 below occurring during the Period of Insurance
provided that
A) as regards Item 3 the loss or damage is due to robbery or attempt thereat
B) as regards Item 5 the loss or damage is due to theft or attempt thereat and
C) the Company's liability in respect of any one occurrence or number of occurrences arising directly or indirectly from any one source or original cause shall not exceed the relevant Limit of Liability

| Item No | Limit of Liability any one loss |
|---|---|
| 1  Money as described in Interpretation 1A | |
| A) in the Insured's Premises during Working Hours or in transit or in a bank night safe and thereafter within bank premises until at the bank's risk or at any of the Insured's contract sites during Working Hours | As shown in the Schedule |
| B) in the Insured's Premises out of Working Hours | |
| 1) in locked safes or strongrooms as shown in the Schedule | As shown in the Schedule |
| 2) in all other locked safes or strongrooms | £1,000 in total |
| 3) not in a locked safe or strongroom | £250 |

C) in the Insured's residence or that of any of the
Insured's directors partners or employees
1) while in a locked safe or while an adult is in the
residence                                                          £500
2) otherwise                                                       £250

2   Money as described in Interpretation 1B                        £250,000

3   Clothing and personal effects (not exceeding £25 per
person in personal money) belonging to the Insured or
any of the Insured's directors partners or employees
while engaged in the Business                                      £250 per person

4   Stamped or impressed National Insurance Cards                  Unlimited

5   Any postal franking machine safe strongroom or any
container or waistcoat used for the carriage of Money
belonging to the Insured or for which the Insured is
responsible                                                        Unlimited

## Exclusions

The Company shall not be liable for
1) loss by theft by any director partner or employee of the Insured not discovered
within seven working days of the occurrence

2) shortage due to error or omission

3) loss from an unattended vehicle

4) loss due to the use of counterfeit Money

5) loss or damage arising from riot or civil commotion in Northern Ireland

6) loss or damage not within Great Britain Northern Ireland the Republic of Ireland
the Channel Islands or the Isle of Man

7) loss destruction or damage directly occasioned by pressure waves caused by
aircraft or other aerial devices travelling at sonic or supersonic speeds

8) loss or damage arising from war invasion act or foreign enemy hostilities
(whether war be declared or not) civil war rebellion revolution insurrection or
military or usurped power

9) loss or destruction of or damage to any property whatsoever or any loss or
expense whatsoever resulting or arising therefrom or any consequential loss

directly or indirectly caused by or contributed to by or arising from
1) ionising radiations or contamination by radioactivity from any nuclear fuel or from any nuclear waste from the combustion of nuclear fuel
2) the radioactive toxic explosive or other hazardous properties of any explosive nuclear assembly or nuclear component thereof

**Interpretations**

1 Money shall mean
A Cash bank notes currency notes uncrossed cheques (including uncrossed giro cheques giro cash cheques and travellers' cheques but excluding pre-signed blank cheques) uncrossed bankers' drafts uncrossed postal orders uncrossed money orders current postage and revenue stamps National Insurance stamps (not fixed to cards) National Savings stamps bills of exchange luncheon vouchers consumer redemption vouchers Holiday with Pay stamps gift tokens trading stamps

B crossed cheques (including crossed giro cheques and drafts but excluding pre-signed blank cheques) crossed bankers' drafts crossed postal orders crossed money orders unused units in franking machines National Savings Certificates Premium Bonds credit company sales vouchers VAT purchase invoices
belonging to the Insured or for which the Insured is responsible and pertaining to the Business

2 Working Hours shall mean
the period during which the Premises are actually occupied for Business purposes and during which the Insured or those of the Insured's employees who are entrusted with Money are in the Premises or on the Insured's contract sites

## Special Conditions

It is a condition precedent to the Company's liability for loss or damage that

A) in respect of any Intruder Alarm System installed at the Premises

1) a maintenance contract is maintained in force during the currency of the Policy with the installing contractor or such other contractor as is agreed in writing by the Company

2) the Business Premises are not left unattended unless

A) the Intruder Alarm System is tested and set in its entirety and where the equipment permits any Central Station to which the Intruder Alarm System is connected has acknowledged the setting signal and

B) as far as the Insured or his representative is aware the Intruder Alarm Signal is in full and efficient working order

3) the agreement of the Company is obtained in writing before replacing extending or otherwise altering the Intruder Alarm System

4) the Company is notified immediately and in writing if

A) the Insured receive written notification from a Police Authority that they may be withdrawing response to alarm calls or

B) the Insured is required to abate a nuisance under the Code of Practice on Noise from Audible Intruder Alarms 1983 or by the Force policy issued by the Chief Constable

B) whenever the Premises are left unattended

1) all locks bolts and other protective devices are in full operation

2) all keys (including those relating to any part of the Intruder Alarm System) other than keys to safes or strongrooms containing money are

A) removed from the Business Premises or

B) placed within a locked safe or strongroom the keys to which are themselves removed from the Business Premises

C) out of working hours all keys and notes of combination lock letters and numbers of safes and strongrooms containing Money are removed from the Business Premises

Interpretation
Intruder Alarm System shall be deemed to include all lines and equipment used to transmit the signals to and from the Premises

**2 Contribution**
If at the time of any claim under this Section the Insured is or would but for the existence of this Policy be entitled to indemnity under any other policy or policies the Company shall not be liable except in respect of any excess beyond the amount which would have been payable under such other policy or policies had this Section not been effected

# Fidelity Insurance

The Company will indemnify the Insured
1  against loss of money or goods belonging to or held in trust by the Insured

caused by any act of fraud or dishonesty committed by any Employee
described in the Schedule in connection with his employment by the Insured in
the Business during the currency of
A) this insurance after the Commencement Date applicable to such Employee
   or
B) any previous fidelity insurance effected by the Insured but not discovered
during the period stipulated in such insurance but
    1) only to the extent that such loss would have been insured had such
       insurance remained in force
    2) only if fidelity insurance has been maintained continuously in force
       and discovered not later than twenty four months after the termination of
A) the insurance in respect of such Employee
   or
B) this Policy
whichever occurs first

Provided that the Company shall not be liable for loss of interest or
consequential loss of any kind

2  for auditors' fees incurred with the Company's written consent to substantiate
   the amount of a claim

The liability of the Company including liability for auditors' fees shall not exceed
A) the Specific Limit of Indemnity in respect of any one Employee or category
   of Employee
B) the Aggregate Limit of Indemnity for all Employees for all losses discovered
   within a Period of Insurance

On notification of a claim the Specific and Aggregate Limits of Indemnity for
Employees not the subject of such claim shall be maintained provided the
Insured agrees to pay the additional premium The reinstated amount shall
apply only to acts of fraud or dishonesty committed subsequent to the date of
notification

**Exclusion**
The Company shall not be liable for the amount of the Insured's Contribution

**Interpretations**

Insured's Contribution shall mean the first part of each and every loss borne by
the Insured as specified in the Schedule

Employee shall mean any person normally resident within the Geographical
Limits who is under a contract of employment or apprenticeship with the
Insured

Geographical Limits shall mean Great Britain Northern Ireland the Channel
Islands the Isle of Man and the Republic of Ireland

## Special Conditions

### The Insured's Duties
The Insured shall
A) take references in respect of each Employee in accordance with the information given in the Proposal
B) observe the System of Check declared in the Proposal
C) not continue to trust any Employee with money or goods after the Insured has knowledge of any material fact bearing on the honesty of the Employee unless the Company is advised and the Company's written approval obtained

### Recoveries
Any money of the Employee in the Insured's hands and any money which but for the Employee's dishonesty would have been due to the Employee from the Insured shall be deducted from the amount otherwise payable under this insurance The Insured and the Company shall share any other recovery (excluding insurance and reinsurance and any counter-security taken by the Company) made by either on account of any loss in the proportion that the amount of the loss borne by each bears to the total amount of the loss

### Application of Limits of Indemnity
Irrespective of the number of Periods of Insurance during which this Policy (and any Policy issued in substitution therefor) shall remain in force the Company's liability for any one claim shall not exceed the Specific Limit of Indemnity in respect of any one Employee or category of Employee nor the Aggregate Limit of Indemnity for all Employees

# Property Damage Insurance

If any of the Property Insured described in the Schedule suffers Damage at the Premises by any of the Covers insured the Company will in accordance with the provisions of the insurance pay to the Insured the amount of loss or at its option reinstate or replace such property
provided that the Company's liability in any one Period of Insurance shall not exceed in the whole the total sum insured or in respect of any item its sum insured or any other stated limit of liability

For the purpose of this insurance Damage shall mean loss destruction or damage

### Covers
The following are the Covers insured except as otherwise stated in the Schedule
1   A **Fire** excluding Damage
    1) by explosion resulting from fire
    2) to property caused by its undergoing any process involving the application of heat

B **Explosion** excluding Damage
  1) caused by the bursting of any boiler economiser or other vessel machine or apparatus belonging to or under the control of the Insured in which internal pressure is due to steam only
  2) to any vessel machine or apparatus or its contents resulting from the explosion thereof
  but this shall not exclude Damage caused by explosion of
  – any boiler
  – gas
  used for domestic purposes only
C **Lightning**
D **Aircraft** or other aerial devices or articles dropped therefrom

2 **Earthquake** excluding Damage caused by fire

3 **Riot civil commotion strikers locked-out workers or persons taking part in labour disturbance or malicious persons** excluding Damage
  1) arising from confiscation or destruction by order of the government or any public authority
  2) arising from cessation of work
  3) A) in the course of theft or attempted theft
     B) in respect of any building which is empty or not in use
     directly caused by malicious persons not acting on behalf of or in connection with any political organisation

4 **Storm of flood** excluding Damage
  1) attributable solely to change in the water table level
  2) caused by frost subsidence ground heave or landslip
  3) to fences gates and moveable property in the open

5 **Escape of water from any tank apparatus or pipe** excluding Damage
  1) by water discharged or leaking from an automatic sprinkler installation
  2) in respect of any building which is empty or not in use
6 **Impact by any road vehicle** (including any fork lift truck or other industrial vehicle) or animal

7 **Accidental escape of water from any automatic sprinkler installation** excluding Damage
  1) by freezing in any building which is empty or not in use
  2) by heat caused by fire

8 **Theft (which shall be deemed to include attempted theft)** excluding Damage
  1) which does not involve
     – entry to or exit from a building by forcible and violent means or
     – actual or threatened assault or violence
  2) from any part of the building not occupied by the Insured for the purpose of the Business

3) from the open or from any outbuilding
4) to property in transit
5) to Money and securities of any description
6) glass if more specifically insured

**9  Subsidence ground heave or landslip** excluding Damage
1) arising from the settlement or movement of made-up ground or by coastal or river erosion
2) occurring as a result of the construction demolition structural alteration or structural repair of any property at the Premises
3) arising from normal settlement or bedding down of new structures
4) commencing prior to the granting of cover under this insurance

**10 Any other accident** excluding Damage
1) by any
   A) of the Covers
   B) of the causes expressly excluded from the Covers
   specified in paragraphs 1-9 and 11-16 (whether or not insured)

2) to any property caused by
   A) its own faulty or defective design or materials
   B) inherent vice latent defect gradual deterioration wear and tear
   C) faulty or defective workmanship operational error or omission on the part of the Insured or any of their employees
   but this shall not exclude subsequent Damage which itself results from a cause not otherwise excluded

3) caused by
   A) corrosion rust wet or dry rot shrinkage evaporation loss of weight dampness dryness marring scratching vermin or insects
   B) change in temperature colour flavour texture or finish
   C) joint leakage failure of welds cracking fracturing collapse or overheating of boilers economisers superheaters pressure vessels or any range of steam and feed piping in connection therewith
   D) mechanical or electrical breakdown or derangement in respect of the particular machine apparatus or equipment in which the breakdown or derangement originates
   but this shall not exclude
   1) such Damage which itself results from other Damage and is not otherwise excluded
   2) subsequent Damage which itself results from a cause not otherwise excluded

4) caused by
   A) pollution or contamination
   B) acts of fraud or dishonesty
   C) disappearance unexplained or inventory shortage misfiling or misplacing of information

5) to
   A) a building or structure caused by its own collapse or cracking
   B) moveable property in the open fences and gates by wind rain hail sleet snow flood or dust
   C) property resulting from its undergoing any process of production packing treatment testing commissioning servicing or repair

6) to
   A) property in transit
   B) Money and securities of any description
   C) property or structures in course of construction or erection and materials or supplies in connection with all such property in course of construction or erection

**11 A) Accidental breakage of fixed Glass** by fracture extending through its entire thickness
  B) **Accidental breakage of sanitary earthenware**
  C) **Damage by impact or falling glass to**
   i) the framework and fittings of the ground floor frontage
   ii) goods on display in windows
   excluding
1) breakage
   A) consequent upon alterations to the framework or position of any of the Glass or to sanitary earthenware
   B) consequent upon settlement or expansion or contraction of frames or fittings in buildings under construction and during a period of six months after the date of completion of the buildings
   C) whilst the Premises are empty or disused unless specifically agreed
   D) existing prior to the commencement of this insurance and not subsequently replaced
   E) of
    1) Glass which is bent tinted or stained and fired
    2) lettering or decoration or protective film or alarm foil on Glass unless to comply with the quality recommended in the British Standard Code of Practice BS 6262:1982
    3) Glass which is incorporated in multiple glazing units (other than double glazing) or is frameless on any side
    4) Glass or sanitary earthenware forming part of the Insured's Stock and materials in trade or goods in trust or on commission except in respect of goods on display in windows

**12 Damage by any accident to Specialist Equipment as described in the Schedule** but excluding
1) Damage caused by
   A) wear and tear moth vermin atmospheric or climatic conditions or any gradually operating cause
   B) alterations maintenance repairs or any process of cleaning or restoring

    C) delay confiscation or detention by order of any Government or Public
       Authority
    D) counterfeit substitute or foreign coins
    E) mechanical or electrical breakdown or derangement
  2) breakage of electrical valves bulbs or tubes unless forming part of the
     property and fixed therein and happening as the result of Damage to such
     property
  3) the contents of machines unless such contents are shown in the Schedule
  4) depreciation contamination consequential loss or consequential damage of
     any kind or description
  5) Damage consequent upon any person obtaining any property by deception

**13 Oil** escaping from a fixed heating installation or apparatus connected therewith
excluding the cost of replacing the oil

**14 Falling trees** or parts thereof excluding Damage caused by felling or lopping
by or on behalf of the Insured

**15 Damage to Buildings** caused by falling television or radio receiving aerials
aerial fittings and masts

**16 Accidental Damage** for which the Insured is responsible to the underground
water gas and drain pipes or electricity cable extending from the Buildings to
the public mains

**Insured's Contribution**
This insurance does not cover the Insured's Contribution (as shown below or as
otherwise specified in the Schedule) being the first part of each and every loss to
be borne by the Insured at each separate premises as ascertained after the
application of all terms and conditions of the insurance including the
Underinsurance Provision
A  Cover 9 (Subsidence) if insured                 £1,000
B  All other Covers                             £  100

# Exclusions

This insurance does not cover

A **Marine Policies**
   Damage to property which at the time of the happening of the Damage is
   insured by or would but for the existence of this insurance be insured by any
   marine policy or policies except in respect of any excess beyond the amount
   which would have been payable under the marine policy or policies had this
   insurance not been effected

B **Sonic Bangs**
Damage caused by pressure waves caused by other aerial devices travelling at sonic or supersonic speeds

C **War and Allied Risks**
Damage occasioned by
1) riot or civil commotion except to the extent that it is specifically insured
2) war invasion act of foreign enemy hostilities (whether war be declared or not) civil war rebellion revolution insurrection or military or usurped power

D **Pollution and Contamination**
Damage caused by pollution or contamination except (unless otherwise excluded) destruction of or damage to the Property Insured caused by
1) pollution or contamination which itself results from any Cover insured (other than Cover 10)
2) any Cover insured (other than Cover 10) which itself results from pollution or contamination

E **Radioactive Contamination**
Damage to any property whatsoever or any loss or expense whatsoever resulting or arising therefrom or any consequential loss directly or indirectly caused by or contributed to by or arising from
1) ionising radiations or contamination by radioactivity from any nuclear fuel or from any nuclear waste from the combustion of nuclear fuel
2) the radioactive toxic explosive or other hazardous properties of any explosive nuclear assembly or nuclear component thereof

F **Northern Ireland**
Damage in Northern Ireland occasioned by or happening through or in consequence of
1) civil commotion
2) any unlawful wanton or malicious act committed maliciously by a person or persons acting on behalf of or in connection with any unlawful association

For the purpose of this exclusion –

Unlawful Association means any organisation which is engaged in terrorism and includes an organisation which at any relevant time is a proscribed organisation within the meaning of the Northern Ireland (Emergency Provisions) Act 1973

Terrorism means the use of violence for political ends and includes any use of violence for the purpose of putting the public or any section of the public in fear

In any action suit or other proceedings where the Company alleges that by reason of the provisions of this exclusion any Damage is not covered by this insurance the burden of proving that such Damage is covered shall be upon the Insured

# Definitions of Property

## Property Insured
- Buildings
- General Contents
- Stock
- Other property or interests

at the Premises excluding while in the open or in any out-building unless such outbuilding has been specified in the Schedule

all as defined below or more fully described in the Schedule and all being the property of the Insured or for which they are responsible but excluding
- property which is more specifically insured
- unless specifically notified to and accepted by the Company as insured
  A) land roads pavements piers jetties bridges culverts or excavations
  B) livestock growing crops or trees

## Buildings
- buildings (being built mainly of brick stone concrete or other non-combustible materials unless otherwise stated in the Schedule)
- landlord's fixtures and fittings in and on the buildings
- small outside buildings extensions annexes gangways
- walls gates and fences
- services which shall mean
    telephone gas and water mains electrical instruments meters piping cabling and the like and the accessories thereon extending from the buildings to the perimeter of the premises or to the public mains (including those under ground)

## Tenant's Improvements
- tenant's improvements alterations and decorations

## General Contents
- machinery plant fixtures fittings and other trade equipment
- all office equipment and other contents
- patterns models moulds plans and designs
- computer records documents manuscripts and business books for an amount not exceeding £25,000 in respect of any one loss
- in so far as they are not otherwise insured
    directors' partners' and employees' personal effects including clothing pedal cycles tools instruments and the like for an amount not exceeding £500 per person
  but any cover granted under this insurance for Damage by theft or attempted theft shall not apply to
    personal effects partly or wholly of precious metal jewellery watches furs contact lenses portable electronic entertainment equipment cameras Money and securities of any description

- to the extent that they are not otherwise insured
    motor vehicles motor chassis and their contents
- satellite dishes

## Money
- cash bank notes currency notes cheques bankers' drafts postal orders money orders current postage stamps and revenue stamps National Insurance stamps National Savings stamps and certificates holiday savings stamps luncheon vouchers credit company sales vouchers VAT purchase invoices Premium Bonds bills of exchange giro cheques and drafts gift tokens trading stamps unused units of franking machines consumer redemption vouchers and credit cards

## Stock
- Stock and materials in trade work in progress and finished goods

## Glass
- Normal flat annealed glass including toughened and laminated glass and mirrors including lettering thereon unless otherwise shown in the Schedule

## Designation of Property
Where necessary the item heading under which any property is insured shall be determined by the designation under which such property appears in the Insured's books

# The Insurance Provided

**In respect of Buildings Tenants' Improvements and General Contents** (other than motor vehicles directors' partners' and employees' personal effects and Specialist Equipment if insured separately)

the Company will pay —

A **the cost of reinstatement** being
- where the property is destroyed the cost of rebuilding or in the case of General Contents the cost of its replacement by similar property
- where the property is damaged the cost of repairing or restoring the damaged portions
to a condition substantially the same as but not better or more extensive than its condition when new

B **the cost of complying with Public Authorities' requirements** being
such additional cost of reinstatement of the property as may be incurred with the Company's consent in complying with Building Regulations or local

authority or other statutory requirements first imposed upon the Insured following the Damage provided that the reinstatement is completed within twelve months of the occurrence of the Damage or within such further time as the Company may in writing allow

C **the cost of removing debris** being
the cost incurred with the Company's consent in removing debris dismantling demolishing shoring up and propping portions of the property but excluding any costs or expenses
1) incurred in removing from outside the site of the Premises at which the Damage has occurred other than from the area immediately adjacent to that site
2) arising from pollution or contamination of property not covered by this insurance

D **the cost of professional fees** being
those necessarily incurred in the reinstatement of the property but not for preparing any claims

The undernoted provisions apply

1 **Public Authorities' Requirements**
The Company shall not be liable in respect of cost B for
– requirements relating to undamaged property or undamaged portions of property other than foundations (unless foundations are specifically excluded from the insurance)
– any rate tax duty development or other charge or assessment which may arise out of capital appreciation as a result of complying with any of the regulations or requirements referred to

2 **Partial Damage**
Where Damage occurs to only part of the property the Company's liability shall not exceed the amount which the Company would have been liable to pay had the property been wholly destroyed

3 **Reinstatement on Another Site**
The work of reinstatement may be carried out wholly or partially upon another site and in any manner suitable to the requirements of the Insured provided that it does not increase the Company's liability

4 **Insurable Amount**
For the purpose of the Underinsurance Provision the Insurable Amount shall be the Day One Reinstatement Value
Day One Reinstatement Value shall mean
the total of the insured costs A B C and D in reinstating the Property Insured to a condition substantially the same as when new at the level of costs applying at the commencement of the Period of Insurance

## 5 Alternative Basis of Settlement

The Company's liability shall be limited to the Alternative Basis of Settlement (as defined below)

A) until the cost of reinstatement has actually been incurred
B) if the work of reinstatement if not carried out as quickly as is reasonably practicable
C) if at the time of its Damage the property is covered by any other insurance effected by or on behalf of the Insured and such other insurance is not on the identical basis of reinstatement defined in cost A
D) if in the Schedule it is stated that the Alternative Basis of Settlement applies

Under the Alternative Basis of Settlement the Company will pay the value of the property at the time of its destruction or the amount of the damage including the cost of

– complying with Public Authorities' requirements
– removing debris
– professional fees

as defined in costs B C and D above and subject to the provisions and exceptions applying to those costs

For the purpose of the Underinsurance Provision the Insurable Amount shall be the total of the value at the time of the Damage of the Property Insured by the item and the additional costs B C and D

### In respect of computer records documents manuscripts and business books

the Company will pay —
A) the value of the materials as stationery
B) the clerical labour and computer time expended in reproducing such computer records or writing up such documents
C) the costs necessarily and reasonably incurred in connection with the reproduction of any information to be recorded but excluding the value to the Insured of the information and subject to the Company's liability not exceeding the limit stated in the definition of General Contents

### In respect of Specialist Equipment if insured

the Company will pay —
– where the property is destroyed the cost of its replacement by similar property
– where the property is damaged the cost of repairing or restoring the damaged portions to a condition substantially the same as but not better or more extensive than its condition when new
including the cost of removing debris (as defined in cost C)

### In respect of Stock and other insured property not specifically provided for

the Company will pay

the value of the property at the time of its destruction or the amount of the damage including the cost of removing debris (as defined in cost C)

The undernoted provisions apply

### 1 Seasonal Increase
The sum insured in respect of Stock shall be increased by 50% for the months of November and December and for 31 days immediately preceding Easter Day This provision shall not apply to the Stock in Transit Extension

### 2 Insurable Amount
For the purpose of the Underinsurance Provision the Insurable Amount shall be the value at the time of Damage of the Property insured by the Item

### 3 In respect of Tobacco
the liability of the Company shall be limited in respect of Tobacco (including cigars and cigarettes) to an amount not exceeding in any Period of Insurance the sum of £500 or as otherwise specified in the Schedule

### In respect of Glass
the Company will pay
A) the cost of replacing the broken Glass with glass
   1) of similar quality or cost or
   2) of the quality recommended in the British Standard Code of Practice BS6262 : 1982 where applicable to certain glazing risk areas as defined in such Code
   or at its option the Company will pay to the Insured the cost of such replacement less the value of any salvage
B) the reasonable cost of any necessary boarding up or temporary glazing pending replacement of the broken glass and the reasonable cost of removing and refixing window fittings and other obstacles to replacement
C) in respect of Damage by impact or falling glass to the framework and fittings of the ground floor frontage or goods on display in the windows or at its option repair reinstate or replace to indemnify the Insured in respect of the broken or damaged items provided that the liability of the Company for any one occurrence shall not exceed £500

### In respect of Rent of Buildings which suffer Damage
the Company will pay —
A) if the loss relates to rent receivable by the Insured
   – the actual reduction in rent received solely in consequence of the Damage
B) if the loss relates to rent payable by the Insured
   – the amount of rent which continues to be payable by the Insured in respect of the Building or portions of the Building whilst unfit for occupation in consequence of the Damage
but the Company's liability shall be limited to the loss suffered within the period of rent insured (as specified in the Schedule) which commences from the date of the Damage

The undernoted provision applies
**Insurable Amount**
For the purpose of the Underinsurance Provision the Insurable Amount shall be
the annual rent receivable (or in the case of B) above the annual rent payable) at
the commencement of the Period of Insurance such amount to be proportionately
increased to correspond with the period of rent insured where that period
exceeds twelve months

# General Provisions applicable to all items

## Underinsurance
If at the time of the Damage
– the Declared Value by the relative item on Buildings Tenant's or General
  Contents or
– the sum insured by the relative item on other property or interests
– the limit in respect of Tobacco
is less than the Insurable Amount the amount otherwise payable shall be
proportionately reduced

Declared Value shall mean
the base value shown in brackets below the sum insured such value excluding
any provision for inflation but if the loss is settled under the Alternative Basis of
Settlement the Declared Value shall be 115% of the base value shown or if no
base value is shown it shall be deemed to be the sum insured

### Reinstatement by the Company
The Company may at its own option reinstate or replace any property destroyed
or damaged without being bound to reinstate exactly or completely but only as
circumstances permit and in reasonably sufficient manner
The Insured shall at their own expense produce and provide the Company with
all such plans documents books and information as the Company may
reasonably require

### Extinguishment Expenses
The Company will pay the reasonable costs incurred by the Insured in refilling
fire extinguishing appliances and replacing used sprinkler heads solely in
consequence of insured Damage to the Property Insured

### Theft Cover Extension
Any cover granted under this insurance in respect of Theft or attempted theft
includes
A) the cost of repairing Damage to the Buildings (whether or not the Buildings
   are insured hereunder) if the Insured is responsible for the repairs and the
   Damage is not otherwise insured
B) the reasonable expenses (not exceeding £500) incurred in necessarily

replacing locks to the Buildings or safes or strongrooms therein consequent upon the theft or attempted theft (as insured) of keys from such building or from the residence of any of the authorised keyholding directors partners or employees of the Insured

## Stock in Transit Extension

In the event of Damage by any cause to Stock while

1   being loaded upon carried by or unloaded from any vehicle owned or operated by the Insured anywhere in Great Britain Northern Ireland the Republic of Ireland the Channel Islands or the Isle of Man

2   at exhibitions which do not exceed 7 days duration

the Company will by payment or at its option by repair reinstatement or replacement indemnify the Insured in respect of such Damage provided that the liability of the Company in respect of any claim arising out of any one event shall not exceed the limit per vehicle (except as provided for in A B and C below) and in respect of property at exhibition premises shall not exceed £1,000 in any one Period of Insurance
Limit per vehicle                                          £1,000
Number of Insured's Own Vehicles                           One

In addition the Company will indemnify the Insured in respect of
A) additional costs reasonably incurred in
    1) transhipping Stock to another vehicle delivering it to the original destination or returning it to the place of despatch following Damage to the Stock or an accident to the conveying vehicle
    2) removal of debris following Damage to the Stock or an accident to the conveying vehicle
    3) reloading on to any vehicle any Stock if it falls from such vehicle

Limit of Liability in respect of all claims arising out of
any one event                                             £1,000
B) Damage to sheets ropes packing materials dunnage securing chains and toggles owned by the Insured or in the charge or control of the Insured while carried on any such vehicle

Limit of Liability in respect of all claims arising out of
any one event                                             £1,000

C) Damage to the personal effects belonging to the driver or attendant while carried by any such vehicle in the course of the employment of the driver or attendant with the Insured

Limit of Liability in respect of all claims arising out of
any one event for any one person                                £100

**Exclusions**
The Company shall not be liable in respect of
1  Loss of market delay or any consequential loss

2  Loss resulting from dishonesty or insolvency of persons to whom goods are
   entrusted

3  Destruction of or damage to glass china marble earthenware scientific
   instruments furniture antiques curios sculptures work of art pictures prints
   drawings engravings and goods of a brittle nature unless caused by fire theft or
   as a direct result of collision or overturning of the conveying vehicle

4  Loss of sheets ropes packing materials dunnage securing chains and toggles
   as a result of disappearance or shortage if such loss is only revealed when an
   inventory is made unless such loss is the result of an incident recorded by the
   Insured

5  Stock warehoused at a rental or under contract for storage and distribution

6  Money and securities

7  Jewellery watches furs cameras radios televisions record players cassette
   players and video equipment belonging to vehicle drivers or attendants

8  Stock carried by or despatched by the Insured for hire or reward

9  Destruction or damage to stock arising as a result of packing which was
   inadequate to withstand normal handling during transit
Loss destruction or damage to stock
A) due to insufficient labelling or incorrect addressing
B) in any vehicle which is being used outside the normal course of the Business
   for social domestic or pleasure purposes
C) in open vehicles owned or operated by the Insured caused by atmospheric or
   climatic conditions unless the stock is protected by vehicle sheets
D) left in any vehicle for the night except where such vehicle is left closed and
   locked and either
   1) garaged in a building which is securely closed and locked
      or
   2) left in a compound secured by locked gates

The first £50 of each and every loss

# General Memoranda

## Property at other locations
Subject to all the provisions and exclusions the cover granted by this insurance is extended to apply to the undernoted Property Insured whilst removed from the premises as indicated below except that
1) the insurance applies only in so far the property is not otherwise insured
2) any cover granted in respect of Damage by theft or attempted theft shall not apply under this extension
3) this extension applies only to Damage occurring within Great Britain Northern Ireland and the Republic of Ireland
4) the Company's liability for any one loss shall not exceed the limit stated

| Property and Location | Limit of liability for any one loss |
|---|---|
| A  Computer records documents manuscripts and business books at any location and whilst in transit | The limit stated in the General definition |
| B  Other property (excluding vehicles licensed for road use) at any location to which the property has been temporarily removed for cleaning renovation repair or other similar purposes and whilst in transit | 15% of the relative sum insured but in no case exceeding £250,000 |

## Automatic Reinstatement after a Loss
In the absence of written notice by the Insured or the Company to the contrary within 30 days of the occurrence of any Damage the Company's liability shall not be reduced by the amount of any loss and the Insured shall pay the appropriate additional premium for such automatic reinstatement of cover
provided that in respect of Damage by theft or attempted theft (if insured) the automatic reinstatement shall apply on the first occasion only in each Period of Insurance

## Index Linking
If shown in the Schedule as applicable the Company will adjust the sum insured (and the Declared Value where appropriate) by each item on Buildings Tenant's Improvements General Contents and Stock in line with suitable indices of costs and the premium for renewal will be based on the adjusted amounts

## Transfer of Interest
If at the time of any insured Damage to any building insured the Insured shall have contracted to sell their interest in the building and the purchase is subsequently completed the purchaser shall be entitled on completion of the

purchase to the benefit of this insurance in respect of such Damage if and so far as the property is not otherwise insured by the purchaser or on the purchaser's behalf against such Damage without prejudice to the rights and liabilities of the Insured or the Company under this insurance up to the date of completion

**Workmen**
Workmen are allowed on the Premises for the purpose of effecting repairs and minor structural and other alterations and also for general maintenance purposes and the like without prejudice to this insurance

**Risk Protections**
A **Automatic Sprinkler and Fire Alarm Installations**
(Applicable if a reduced premium rate is allowed on account of such an installation or if the insurance covers Damage by the accidental escape of water from a sprinkler installation)
The Insured shall
1) take all reasonable steps to
   A) prevent frost and other damage to the installations
   and in so far as it is their responsibility
   B) maintain the installations (including the automatic external alarm signal) in efficient condition
   C) maintain ready access to the water supply control facilities
2) in the event that changes repairs or alterations to the installations are proposed notify the Company in writing and obtain its prior agreement in writing
3) allow the Company access to the Premises at all reasonable times for the purpose of inspecting the installations
4) carry out the routine tests laid down by the Company and remedy promptly any defect revealed by a test

In the event that alterations or repairs become necessary to the automatic sprinkler installation the Company may at its option suspend any cover which is granted against Damage by the accidental escape of water from the installation until the alterations or repairs have been carried out and approved by the Company
Notice of any such action will be given by the Company in writing

B **Fire Extinguishing Appliances**
(Applicable if a reduced premium rate is allowed on account of the appliances)
The Insured shall maintain all fire extinguishing appliances in efficient working order

C **Intruder Alarms**
(Applicable to any cover granted in respect of Damage by theft or attempted theft)
It is a condition precedent to the Company's liability for Damage that

1) in respect of any Intruder Alarm System installed at the Premises
   A) a maintenance contract is maintained in force during the currency of this insurance with the installing contractor or such other contractor as is agreed in writing by the Company

   B) the Premises are not left unattended unless
      1) the Intruder Alarm System is tested and set in its entirety and where the equipment permits any Central Station to which the Intruder Alarm System is connected has acknowledged the setting signal and
      2) as far as the Insured or their representative is aware the Intruder Alarm System is in full and efficient working order

   C) the agreement of the Company is obtained in writing before replacing extending or otherwise altering the Intruder Alarm System

   D) the Company is notified immediately and in writing if
      1) the Insured receive written notification from the Police Authority that they may be withdrawing response to alarm calls or
      2) The Insured is required to abate a nuisance under the Code of Practice on Noise from Audible Intruder Alarms 1983 or by the force policy issued by the Chief Constable

2) whenever the Premises are left unattended
   A) all locks bolts and other protective devices are in full operation
   B) all keys (including those relating to any part of the Intruder Alarm System) are
      1) removed from the Business Premises
      2) placed within a locked safe or strongroom the keys to which are themselves removed from the Business Premises

For the purpose of this condition Intruder Alarm System shall be deemed to include all lines and equipment used to transmit the signals to and from the Premises

*Reproduced by permission of Sun Alliance Insurance Group*

# APPENDIX H

# Précis of cases

## Anderson v The Commercial Union Assurance Company

*This was a special case stated by an arbitrator*

Anderson was a manufacturer of oil and colour and had a lease on premises at which he had erected a steam engine and the necessary plant and machinery to carry on his business.

Subsequently, he mortgaged the lease and his interest in the premises. He then made a default on the payment of the principal and interest under the mortgage and thus became "tenant at will to the mortgagees".

For some years Anderson had been in the habit of insuring his property with the Commercial Union for periods of 12 months but after the mortgagees had taken possession, he had insured for lesser periods.

On 9 December 1882 there was a fire at the premises and there was serious damage to the building and machinery.

At the time of the fire the machinery was insured with the Commercial Union against damage by fire, the policy being for a period of one month. The policy contained a usual condition to the effect that if insurers thought fit they could reinstate or replace property damaged or destroyed instead of paying the amount of the loss or damage.

After the fire the mortgagees decided to take possession of the premises and they put an end to Anderson's tenancy.

When the buildings were reinstated, the Commercial Union elected to reinstate the machinery within the terms of its policy and this it did within a reasonable time.

The mortgagees had, however, taken possession of the premises and Anderson could not now get possession of the machinery as he could not get permission to go onto the premises.

Anderson therefore contended that he was entitled to be recouped in the amount of the loss or damage in money.

The Commercial Union argued that it had fulfilled its obligations under the policy because it exercised its right to reinstate or replace the machinery.

Commercial Union argued further that Anderson had not at the time of insuring informed it of the precarious nature of his tenure and it contended that this was such a concealment of fact as to make the policy void.

Mr Justice Manesty said that he thought that the

> sole question raised by the case on the subject of the indemnity was whether the Company having exercised their option to reinstate the subject matter of the insurance, the Plaintiff could, under the circumstances insist upon their repaying him the amount of his loss in money.

Mr Justice Wills, concurring, also saw this as the essential point and they both agreed that the Commercial Union had the right to reinstate, it had exercised that right, it had therefore within the terms of the policy afforded an indemnity to Anderson and it was not to be called upon to make a further payment or reinstate elsewhere.

On the question of the alleged non-disclosure of a material fact, both Mr Justice Manesty and Mr Justice Wills considered that it was not necessary to make a decision upon that point but speaking obiter Mr Justice Manesty said that he would be inclined to decide that point also in favour of the company and Mr Justice Wills said "It should therefore have been disclosed by the Insured for all the circumstances were material that a reasonable man would require to know before he decided if he would accept the venture".

# Bacon v Cooper (Metals) Ltd

*Indemnity (third party)*

Peter Bacon operated a piece of equipment known as a "fragmentiser" in connection with his business as a scrap metal dealer.

In the course of his dealings he entered into a contract with Cooper (Metals) Ltd whereby it sold to him a quantity of pressed and sheared steel. A bale of metal was delivered to Bacon's premises but during processing within the plant the main rotor of the fragmentiser was broken because the bale of material had contained a large lump of steel.

Judgement on liability was given against Cooper (Metals) Ltd on the grounds of breach of contract on the basis that the material supplied did not correspond with the contract description, was not of merchantable quality and not fit for the purpose for which it was supplied.

In the context of this book the important point decided by the court was the basis upon which Bacon should be "indemnified", ie what was the correct basis of measuring the loss in respect, *inter alia*, of the rotor?

The rotor had been in use for some time and it was argued that as its remaining life was three and a quarter years out of a total expected life of seven years, the plaintiff (Bacon) should contribute towards the cost of the replacement rotor.

Judge Cantley concluded that this was inappropriate, quoting with approval from *Banco de Portugal v Waterlow* (1932), *Harbutts Plasticine v Wayne Tank* (1970) and *The Gazelle* (1844).

Bacon was therefore able to recover the full cost of replacing the rotor because its replacement was the only sensible method of repair which could have been adopted in the circumstances of the case.

# Banque Financière de la Cité SA v Westgate Insurance Company Limited

## Utmost good faith

The hearing of this appeal occupied 24 working days and was an appeal from the lower courts decision in four actions, described by Slade LJ as "issues of fact and law of considerable complexity and interest".

A Spanish businessman persuaded a number of banks to make loans to four companies which he controlled. The securities for those loans consisted of valuable gems and credit insurance policies. The credit insurance policies contained clauses excluding policy liability for claims arising out of fraud.

The manager of a firm of insurance brokers was employed by the Spaniard to place the credit insurance. He attempted to do this by placing a percentage of the risk with a number of insurers. Unfortunately, before the critical time prior to the date of the first loan, he was unable to obtain 100 per cent cover. He therefore obtained a 14 day temporary cover for the shortfall. He did not, on the cover note issued, make it clear that the shortfall had been made up by way of temporary cover and, as a result, the loan went ahead.

An underwriter for the temporary insurer was aware of the situation, although it must be emphasised was not in any way involved in a fraud.

There then followed a complex series of events leading to further insurances and loans, a combination of loans and placings of insurance cover.

The companies controlled by the Spaniard eventually defaulted on the loans, the valuable gems were found to be worth a small part of the valuation figures and the Spaniard himself disappeared with the money. The insurer denied liability, relying upon the exclusion clauses relating to fraud and actions were brought by various banks against the insurance broker who accepted liability up to the level of its liability insurance cover.

The banks, of course, wished to recover the balance of their losses and claimed under four separate headings. Only one of those headings is relevant to our consideration, namely that the insurer (now owned by the Westgate Insurance Company) owed a duty of care to the lending banks, and that when it came to its notice that the broker's employee had deceived the bank in the early stages in respect of one credit insurance, then the insurer should have disclosed to them that deceit.

The trial judge found that the duty of utmost good faith was reciprocal between the insured and insurer; that principle was not disputed. The trial judge also decided however, that the deception of the banks was a material fact and the banks, therefore, were entitled to damages for that breach.

The Court of Appeal varied that decision, although, of course, it confirmed that the obligation to disclose material facts was a mutual and absolute obligation on both parties to the insurance contract.

The Court of Appeal also found that by failing to disclose the deception, the insurer was indeed in breach of the duty of utmost good faith to the banks. The court found in addition, however, that as that duty originally arose in the Court of Equity, it did not give the right to any damages. The only right afforded by the principle of utmost good faith, is that the aggrieved party may rescind the contract.

# Carlill v Carbolic Smoke Ball Company

*Contract — offer and acceptance*

The Carbolic Smoke Ball Company was the proprietor of a medical prep-
aration called the Carbolic Smoke Ball and on 13 November 1891 it published the following advertisement in the Pall Mall Gazette.

> £100 reward will be paid by the Carbolic Smoke Ball Co to any person who
> contracts the increasing epidemic influenza, colds, or any diseases caused by
> taking cold, after having used the ball three times daily for two weeks according
> to the printed directions supplied with each ball. £1000 is deposited with the
> Alliance Bank, Regent Street, showing our sincerity in the matter. During the last
> epidemic of influenza many thousand Carbolic Smoke Balls were sold as preven-
> tatives against this disease, and in no ascertained case was the disease contracted
> by those using the Carbolic Smoke Ball. One Carbolic Smoke Ball will last a family
> several months, making it the cheapest remedy in the world at the price — 10s
> post free. The ball can be refilled at a cost of 5s. Address; Carbolic Smoke Ball
> Co, 27 Princes Street, Hanover Square, London, W.

Mrs Carlill purchased a smoke ball and used it in accordance with the
instructions from mid November 1891 until 17 January 1892 on which date
she contracted influenza. Her husband then wrote on her behalf to claim
the £100 as advertised.

The Carbolic Smoke Ball Co declined to pay and argued that the advertisement was not a binding promise; that it was a policy of insurance (sic);
that it was a wager or a bet. Lord Justice Lindley discussed these arguments
and said "We are dealing with an express promise to pay £100 in certain
events. There can be no mistake about that at all". He said further

> the offer is to anybody who performed the conditions named in the advertise-
> ment. Anyone who performs the conditions accepts the offer . . .
> We therefore have all the elements which are necessary to form a binding contract
> subject to two observations.

The first point here was the question of vagueness in the advertisement
and this was held not to be vague, and the second point was that of
"consideration".

His Lordship said that he considered that the advantage to the Carbolic
Smoke Ball Co was that the advertising would "produce a sale which is
directly beneficial to them . . . Therefore it appears to me that out of this

transaction emerges an advantage to them which is enough to constitute a consideration''.

The Court of Appeal confirmed the judgement in the lower court, namely that there was a contract and Mrs Carlill was entitled to £100.

# Carter v Boehm

*Utmost good faith*

This is a very basic case in insurance law and has been quoted in many cases subsequent to this date.

The action was brought by Carter on behalf of his brother Governor George Carter against the underwriter Mr Charles Boehm in respect of a policy issued on 16 October 1759 to 16 October 1760 for the benefit of the Governor of Fort Marlborough (George Carter) against the loss of the Fort on the island of Sumatra in the East Indies to a foreign enemy. The event happened: "the Fort was taken by Count D'Estaigne, within the year". The underwriter Charles Boehm argued that there had been a fraud by concealment of circumstances which ought to have been disclosed and in particular the weakness of the fort and the probability of it being attacked by the French.

Part of the evidence in reply to this was that the Governor had £20,000 in effects; and had only insured £10,000 and that he was not guilty of any fault in defending the Fort.

It was argued that all the ". . . circumstances were universally known to every merchant upon the exchange of London" and it was further argued by counsel "that the insured is only obliged to discover facts; not the ideas or speculations which he may entertain, upon such facts".

There was then evidence given regarding the circumstances of correspondence regarding the background of the general warlike activities in the East Indies.

The Lord Mansfield then delivered the resolution of the court during the course of which he said

> Insurance is a contract upon speculation. The special facts, upon which the contingent chance is to be computed, lie most commonly in the knowledge of the insured only: the underwriter trusts to his representation, and proceeds upon confidence that he does not keep back any circumstance in his knowledge, to mislead the underwriter into a belief that the circumstance does not exist, and to induce him to estimate the risque, as if it did not exist.
>
> The keeping back such circumstance is a fraud, and therefore the policy is void. Although the suppression should happen through mistake, without any fraudulent intention; yet still the underwriter is deceived, and the policy is void; because the risque run is really different from the risque understood and intended to be run, at the time of the agreement.
>
> The policy would equally be void, against the underwriter, if he concealed;

as, if he insured a ship on her voyage, which he privately knew to be arrived: and an action would lie to recover the premium.

... Good faith forbids either party from concealing what he privately knows, to draw the other into a bargain, from his ignorance of that fact, and his believing the contrary.

... There are many matters as to which the insured may be innocently silent — he need not mention what the underwriter knows ... [he] ... need not mention what the underwriter ought to know; what he takes upon himself the knowledge of; or what he waves (sic) being informed of.

The underwriter needs not be told what lessens the risque agreed and understood to be run by the express terms of the policy. He needs not to be told general topics of speculation; as for instance — the underwriter is bound to know every cause which may occasion natural perils; as, the difficulty of the voyage — the kind of seasons — the probability of lightning, hurricanes, earthquakes and etc. He is bound to know every cause which may occasion political perils; from the ruptures of States from war, and the various operations of it.

Lord Mansfield's judgement then continued with consideration in detail of the various points of evidence and arguments presented to the court and he concluded that the decision at the original trial, namely that there had been no concealment or breach of good faith, should stand.

# Castellain v Preston

*Indemnity/subrogation*

This is a most important, if not vital, basic case for fire insurance law, which is usually quoted for the statement by Brett LJ in respect of the principle of indemnity, but in fact most of the judgements given by Brett and Cotton LJJ were concerned with the matter of subrogation which is, of course, integral to the concept of indemnity.

It is recommended that the full judgement should be read.

This case was an appeal from a judgement of Chitty J in the Queen's Bench Division whose decision was reversed.

Preston and others owned property including a house which on 31 July 1878 they contracted to sell to their tenant Rayner for £3100 and a deposit was paid. The contract provided that completion should be within two years from the date of the contract.

On 15 August 1878 a fire occurred damaging part of the property, "the house was burnt down" and Preston made a claim against the insurers — the London, Liverpool, and Globe Insurance Company. The claim was settled by payment of £330 on 25 September 1878.

On 25 March 1879 Preston named the day for completion as 5 May 1879. The conveyance was completed on 12 December 1879 and the balance of the purchase money was paid.

The action before the court was by Castellain, suing on behalf of the insurance company of which he was an official, who sought to recover the amount paid in settlement of the claim (plus interest) because Preston had sustained no loss as the purchase price had not been reduced by the extent of the fire damage and the money had not been expended on repairs.

During his judgement Brett LJ said

> The vendors . . . had an insurable interest because they were . . . the legal owners of the property; and because [if the contract was not completed] the vendors if the house was burnt down, would suffer loss . . .

Earlier, speaking obiter during the course of the argument by counsel, Lord Justice Brett had said "it may be said that the goods themselves are insured but the assured can recover only to the extent of his interest".

In continuing his judgement Lord Justice Brett then stated the words which are so often quoted in relation to this case

> The very foundation, in my opinion, of every rule which has been applied to

insurance law is this, namely, that the contract of insurance contained in a marine or fire policy is a contract of indemnity, and of indemnity only, and that this contract means that the assured in case of a loss against which the policy has been made, shall be fully indemnified, but shall never be more than fully indemnified. That is the fundamental principle of insurance and if ever a proposition is brought forward which is at variance with it, that is to say, which either will prevent the assured from obtaining a full indemnity, or which will give to the assured more than a full indemnity, that proposition must certainly be wrong.

The learned Judge considered the doctrine of notice of abandonment in marine insurance "for the purpose of coming to the doctrine of subrogation". He continued

That doctrine [of subrogation] does not arise upon any terms of the contract of insurance; it is only another proposition which has been adopted for the purpose of carrying out the fundamental rule which I have mentioned, and it is a doctrine in favour of the underwriters or insurers in order to prevent the assured from recovering more than a full indemnity; it has been adopted solely for that reason. It is not, to my mind, a doctrine applied to insurance law on the ground that underwriters are sureties. Underwriters are not always sureties. They have rights which are sometimes similar to the rights of sureties but that again is in order to prevent the assured from recovering from them more than a full indemnity . . .

   In order to apply the doctrine of subrogation, it seems to me that the full and absolute meaning of the word must be used, that is to say, the insurer must be placed in the position of the assured. Now it seems to me that in order to carry out the fundamental rule of insurance law, this doctrine of subrogation must be carried to the extent which I am now about to endeavour to express, namely, that as between the underwriter and the assured the underwriter is entitled to the advantage of every right of the assured whether such right consists in contract, fulfilled or unfulfilled or in remedy for tort capable of being insisted on or already insisted on, or in any other right, whether by way of condition or otherwise, legal or equitable, which can be, or has been exercised or has accrued, and whether such right could or could not be enforced by the insurer in the name of the assured by the exercise or acquiring of which right or condition the loss against which the assured is insured, can be, or has been diminished. This seems to me to put this doctrine of subrogation in the largest possible form . . . .

Much of the judgement then continues with consideration of the contractual arrangements for the sale of the property and the way in which subrogation and indemnity are intertwined.

   It was concluded that the insurer was entitled to recover the claim money (and interest) paid to Preston because he had sustained no loss in that the purchase monies had not been diminished.

# Commercial Union Assurance Co v Lister

## *Indemnity/subrogation*

S C Lister owned a silk spinning mill called Wellington Mill at Halifax in Yorkshire.

On 4 December 1873 an explosion of gas occurred in the mill and the mill and its contents were destroyed.

The material damage loss was £50,000 but the insurance cover was for £33,000. In addition, Lister sustained a consequential loss of profits of £6000 which was not insured.

The cause of the explosion was considered to have arisen from the negligence of servants of the Municipal Corporation and Lister began an action against the Corporation to recover his loss.

He did not, however, bring his action for the whole of the loss sustained, ie £56,000, but pursued only his uninsured losses of £23,000.

It was suggested that this was because he was a ratepayer of Halifax and if they lost the action, ie had thus to pay money to him, he would then face an increase in his rates bill!

The action before the court was in the form of an appeal regarding the case as dealt with by the Master of the Rolls who had put Lister under an undertaking to sue for the whole of the amount and not to compromise his action with reference to his position as a ratepayer.

Sir W M James, LJ declined to be drawn into deciding other matters regarding the nature of Lister as a trustee for monies, if any, received from third parties or if he would or would not be in breach of some equitable obligation.

He concluded that the undertaking agreed to by Lister to sue for the whole amount was satisfactory in itself and required no further action by the courts.

The importance of the case as reported lies in the fact that Lister was obliged to sue for the whole amount of the loss sustained and not just for his uninsured loss.

It would appear to follow clearly that if an insurer commences an action to recover from a third party, then the action commenced by the insurer must also be for the full amount of the "common law" loss, ie both insured and uninsured losses.

# Crows Transport Limited v Phoenix Insurance Company Limited

## Transit

The plaintiff, a road haulier, arranged a goods in transit policy with the defendant. The policy incorporated the following endorsement:

> Against all risks of loss of, or damage to the subject matter insured belonging to or in the custody or control of the Insured whilst being loaded upon, carried by or unloaded from the vehicle described herein anywhere within Great Britain or Northern Ireland . . . and whilst temporarily housed during the course of transit whether on or off the vehicles . . .

On the day of the loss, a customer delivered 176 cartons of gramophone records to the premises of Crows Transport. The London manager, Mr McDonald, took them inside and left them at a place he considered to be safe, just outside his office door. He went to lunch and whilst they were in that position seven cartons were stolen. The insurer declined to deal with the claim on the grounds, *inter alia*, that the goods were not in transit.

The County Court Judge held that Crows Transport had taken reasonable steps to safeguard the goods, but he also held that they were "not in the course of transit within the meaning of the policy at the time of the loss". The County Court judge had said:

> . . . the course of transit does not begin until some step has been taken by the hauliers towards loading the goods onto one of their own or a sub-contractor's or other haulier's vehicle.

Lord Denning MR said at appeal:

> I think this is too narrow a construction. It seems to me that goods are temporarily housed during the course of transit if they are housed as an incident of transit such as when they are temporarily housed for a few hours awaiting loading. When you take a parcel to a Post Office or railway station and you hand it over and get a receipt, the goods are in transit from the moment when the Post Office or the railway take them. They are in transit by the . . . vehicles, as the case may be, because from that moment onwards, everything that is done is incidental to that transit.

# Dino Services Limited v The Prudential Insurance Company Limited

*Forcible and violent entry*

Dino Services Ltd was a company that specialised in maintaining, re-building, repairing and selling Ferrari motorcars. The business was effectively controlled by a Mr William Nash.

The company had an insurance policy with Prudential Insurance, providing insurance cover against loss of or damage to property within the premises resulting from, amongst other things, "theft involving entry to the premises by forcible and violent means". The policy also contained a provision that the insured was to take reasonable precautions to safeguard the property.

On Friday 4 October 1985, Mr Nash locked up the premises and drove his car, which was protected by an alarm, to a nearby public house. He left the keys to the business in the glove compartment of the car.

Later he went home leaving the car parked where it was at the public house and the following morning it was gone. When he went to the business premises, he discovered that they had also been entered and a theft had occurred. Entry had been gained by using the keys that had been taken from the motorcar; there was no evidence of force or violence to the premises themselves.

The insurer declined to pay the claim on the grounds that there had been a lack of reasonable care and there had been no violent entry to the premises.

In the initial trial evidence was given that the thieves must have let themselves in at the front door of the premises and switched off the alarm before it operated. The trial judge apparently took the view that Mr Nash was not to be equated with the insured for the purposes of that provision in the policy, and his decision on that point was not challenged on appeal. Not for the only time in his judgement on appeal in this case did Kerr LJ express surprise that a point had not been appealed.

However, the only point at issue was force and violence.

Having considered the case of *Re George and Goldsmiths and General Burglary Insurance Association Limited* (1899), the trial judge found:

> In construing this clause, I have to bear in mind of course, the contra proferentum principle. This was the Defendant's document and, in so far as there are ambiguities, these are to be resolved in favour of the Plaintiff. Now the use of the key

by the thieves was unlawful and the purpose of the use was to injure the Plaintiff's rights in his property by depriving him of it, and I am quite happy to follow the phrase of Bankes LJ in Re Calf and Sun Insurance Office (1920) [that the words to be construed have reference to the character of the act by which the entry is obtained]. It seems, applying the definition in the Oxford English Dictionary, that the theft did involve entry to and exit from the premises by forcible and violent means.

In delivering his appeal decision, Kerr LJ said:

> With great respect, I cannot accept that reasoning. . . I have also already indicated that in my view, the Judge misinterpreted the passage from the Judgement of Bankes LJ on which he relied.

Earlier in his judgement, he had said:

> On that basis, I would take the ordinary meaning of the word "violent" in this context to be that it is intended to convey that the use of some force to effect entry, which may be minimal, such as turning a key in a lock or the turning of a door handle, is accentuated or accompanied by some physical act which can possibly be described as violent in its nature and character

and

> accordingly on that basis, I would not consider for one moment, that the ordinary meaning of the phrase "entry to the premises by forcible and violent means" can be applied to the action of moving the lever of a lock into its open position by means of its proper key and then turning the knob or pushing the door open to go inside.

It was in this judgement that Kerr LJ expressed some surprise that the insurer had not also challenged the definition of "forcible". It will be remembered from the text that force need only be minimal; perhaps if the defendant insurer had challenged both interpretations, a more up-to-date view of force and violence combined would now be available.

# Elcock and Others v Thompson

*Valued policy/indemnity*

Elcock owned property at Easthampstead Park, Wokingham, which was insured against loss or damage by, *inter alia*, fire by a policy with Lloyd's Underwriters dated 22 November 1940. The sum insured on the building was £100,000 and adjoining buildings had a sum insured of £6850, making a total sum insured for all items of buildings on the policy of £106,850.

The policy incorporated the following clause:

> The sum set opposite each item in the specification has been accepted by the Underwriters and the Insured as being the true value of the property insured and in the event of a loss the said property will be assumed to be of such value and will be assessed accordingly.

On 16 May 1947 during the currency of the insurance, the mansion was damaged by fire and there was a debate as to the amount which was payable under the policy as an indemnity. Liability was not denied and this action was in respect of quantum only.

Mr Justice Morris stated during the course of his judgement that:

> Had it been possible to reinstate the damage within a few months of the fire it would have cost £43,252 including professional fees. Further, had a new mansion been built at that time the cost would have been £205,000.

His Honour further agreed that the "actual value of the mansion before the fire was £18,000 and its value after the fire was £12,600".

It is important to note that the work of repair (reinstatement) was *not* carried out.

It was argued for Elcock that underwriters should pay either:

(a) the difference between the agreed value of £100,000 and the value of the mansion after the fire, or
(b) a percentage reduction applied to the agreed value of £100,000 once the difference between actual pre- and post- fire value had been established, or
(c) a sum equal to the cost of reinstating the mansion.

For underwriters it was argued that the indemnity should be based on:
(a) the Marine Insurance Act 1906 s. 69 (3) and limited to the actual depreciation in value caused by the fire, or

(b) the proportion of the agreed value of £100,000 which was the notional cost of reinstatement (£40,252) or the cost of building a new mansion — £205,000.

The agreed value clause was considered to be of prime importance and applied to a partial as well as a total loss.

Judgement was given in favour of Elcock that underwriters should pay an amount calculated as follows:

$$\frac{\text{Reduction in value (£18,000–12,600) £5,400}}{\text{Actual pre-fire value £18,000}} \times \text{£106,850 (total agreed schedule value)}$$

This projected a payment of £32,055.

As previously commented, it should not be overlooked that the notional repair cost of £43,252 was not incurred and it may be that had this cost been incurred the court's decision would have been different.

# Gale v Motor Union Insurance Company

# Loyst v General Accident, Fire and Life Assurance Corporation

*Contribution and exclusion clauses*

This was by way of a special case stated by an arbitrator.

On 4 April 1925 Loyst, with Gale's consent, was driving a motor car owned by Gale and he collided with a motor cyclist. In the County Court the motor cyclist recovered damages and costs totalling £154. 0s. 3d.

At the time of this accident two relevant policies of insurance were in existence.

The first in the name of Gale with the Motor Union was in force from 14 August 1924 to 13 August 1925 in respect of Gale's motor car.

The policy included *(inter alia)* the following words:

> The Company shall indemnify the insured . . . or any relation or friend driving with the insured's consent . . .

The policy contained two conditions immediately relevant to the case.

> Condition 6: The extension of the indemnity to friends or relatives of the insured is conditional upon such friend or relative being a licensed and competent driver and not being insured under any other policy . . .
> Condition 10: If at the time of the happening of any accident, injury, damage or loss covered by this policy, there shall be subsisting any other insurance or indemnity of any nature whatsoever covering the same, whether effected by the insured or by any other persons or firm then the company shall be not be liable to pay or contribute to any such damage or loss more than a rateable proportion of any sum or sums payable in respect thereof for compensation.

The second policy was in the name of Loyst and was with the General Accident and this policy was in force from 31 October 1924 to 30 October 1925 in respect of the motor car owned by Loyst.

The policy afforded an indemnity to the insured (Loyst) in respect of his car and further included the words

> (2) The insured will also be indemnified hereunder whilst personally driving a car not belonging to him provided the insured's own car is not in use at the same time, and provided that there is not other insurance in respect of such car whereby the insured may be indemnified.

There was also a contribution condition in the following terms:

> Condition 5: If at the time of any occurrence of any accident loss or damage there shall be any other indemnity or insurance subsisting whether effected by the insured or by any other person the corporation shall not be liable to pay or contribute more than a rateable proportion of any sums payable in respect of such accident, loss or damage . . . the due observance and fulfilment of the provisions and conditions of this policy . . . shall be a condition to any liability of the corporation to make any payment under this policy.

In due course Gale claimed against the two insurance companies as trustee for Loyst and Loyst claimed against the two insurance companies on his own behalf and it was argued on their behalf that one or other of the policies covered Loyst and that because of condition 10 on the Motor Union policy and condition 5 of the General Accident policy, the two insurers were liable to contribute rateably.

It was argued for the Motor Union that Loyst was insured under another policy and was not covered by its policy.

On behalf of the General Accident it was contended that the liability of one insurer excluded that of the other.

The arbitrator concluded that Loyst satisfied the requirements of condition 6 of the Motor Union policy and it should deal with the claim, and that Loyst's claim against the General Accident failed.

At the appeal Mr Justice Ross in the course of his judgement said

> The terms of these policies are not so clearly expressed as they might be and have naturally given rise to disputes.

He then continued to discuss the various conditions and said

> Accordingly upon the true construction of these various clauses the assured is not deprived of the indemnity altogether, which would be the result if condition 6 of the Motor Union policy and clause 2, sub-clause 2 of the General Accident policy stood alone.

He concluded

> In my opinion the proper award in this case is that the claimants should be paid rateably in respect of this accident by the Motor Company and the Accident Corporation. It is agreed that rateably in the circumstances means that each company pays half. I, therefore, direct that each of the respondents shall pay to the claimants the amount awarded by the arbitrator in equal moieties.

# Leppard v Excess Insurance Co Ltd

*Indemnity*

This was a case before the Court of Appeal on 22/28 February 1979.

The plaintiff, Leppard, owned a cottage at Higher Pennance, Redruth, which he had purchased from his parents-in-law with a view to reselling at a later date.

In September 1974 Leppard arranged a policy of insurance with the Excess with a sum insured of £10,000. A proposal form was completed and this included, *inter alia*, a declaration:

> Declaration.
> "I declare that (1) the sums to be insured represent not less than the full value (the full value is the amount which it would cost to replace the property in its existing form should it be totally destroyed)".

Evidence was given that Leppard had told his broker that the cottage was for sale and that £10,000 was not the asking price. There was, however, no suggestion that the broker was acting as agent for the Excess. The sum insured was increased to £14,000 at the October 1975 renewal date.

On 25 October 1975 the cottage was destroyed by fire and a dispute arose as to the amount payable as an indemnity under the policy.

Leppard argued that he was entitled to the cost of reinstatement and the Excess argued that market value was the correct measure of his loss.

In the lower court an award of £8694 was made, this being a figure mutually agreed as the amount for settlement if the cost of reinstatement was the correct basis. It was said that this sum allowed for betterment but this phrase is not explained or defined.

The essence of Leppard's argument was in the context of the requirement that the sum insured would represent and at all times be maintained at not less than the full value of the buildings.

As one would expect in a case regarding indemnity under a fire insurance policy, *Castellain v Preston* was quoted and there was also reference to the case of Harbutts Plasticine, although it was said that this latter case did not afford much help on the issue before the court.

The Court of Appeal concluded that the correct basis of indemnity in this case was by payment of the market value.

Evidence was given that "just before the fire" Leppard would have been prepared to sell the cottage for as low a sum as £4000.

It had been agreed between the parties that if market value was ruled to be the correct basis for settlement, then the relevant calculation would be to assume a market value of £4500 with a residual value of the land of £1500. Thus the net loss would be £3000.

This was in fact the amount awarded by the Court of Appeal as the court concluded that this represented the loss which had been sustained by Leppard. That is to say it was essentially the sum of money which he had lost because he could no longer sell the property.

# Mackay v London General Insurance Co Ltd

*Proposal form/declaration/concealment*

Mr H M G C Mackay took out a motor policy with the London General Insurance Co Ltd on 24 September 1932.

On 5 November 1932 he was involved in an accident in which he injured two people and subsequently judgement was given against him for a sum of £830 and costs.

Mackay assumed that this claim and judgement would be dealt with by his insurer but it declined liability on the grounds that he had inaccurately and incorrectly answered questions on the proposal form.

One of the questions in the form was: "Has any Office or Underwriter refused, cancelled or declined to accept or renew such insurance, or required an increased premium or special condition?" Mackay had answered "No" in response to this question.

In fact, some three years before when he was 18 (a minor), he had arranged insurance for a motor cycle with the Ocean Accident and Guarantee Corporation and it had stipulated that it would apply a £2.10s excess clause which was its usual practice with minors.

When Mackay had answered "No" to this question on the proposal form he was therefore giving a wrong answer. In giving judgement Mr Justice Swift said "If he had explained the facts I am perfectly certain the insurance would have been accepted — accepted gladly — but as he was so inadvertent as to say "No", he has there made an inaccurate statement".

Another question on the proposal form was: "Have you or your driver ever been convicted or had a motor licence endorsed?" Mackay also answered "No" to this question.

The fact was, however, that a considerable time before he had been fined a sum of 10s because a nut had become loose on the brakes of his motor cycle and it was said of him that he was driving this cycle without efficient brakes. In the circumstances, his answer of "No" was inaccurate. At this point of his judgement Mr Justice Swift went on to say:

> I am quite satisfied that both these answers were quite immaterial; that if he had stated the truth in its full detail this insurance company would have jumped at receiving his premium. They would never have dreamed of rejecting his application, but after they have given him the policy, and after the accident has happened and the liability is incurred, they seize upon these inaccuracies in the proposal form in order to repudiate their liability.

I am extremely sorry for the Plaintiff in this case. I think he has been very badly treated — shockingly badly treated. They have taken his premium. They have not been in the least bit misled by the answers which he has made . . . but I cannot help the position. Sorry as I am for him there is nothing that I can do to help him. The Law is quite plain.

. . . here I am quite satisfied that in the circumstances of this case that these answers were quite immaterial, but, unfortunately for the Plaintiff by the Defendant's form . . . the Plaintiff has contracted that the proposal and declaration shall be the basis of the contract between him and the said Company and in the proposal he has made two answers which I cannot say were accurate.

Much as I sympathise with him, I am bound to say that the Company were within their rights when they repudiated their liability under this policy; and I must dismiss this action with costs.

It must be recognised that this case, whilst taking place in 1935, did and does correctly reflect the law about warranties and warranted statements in proposal forms, but again reference should be made to the current "Statement of Practice" in respect of persons insuring in their private capacity.

# March Cabaret Club and Casino Ltd v London Assurance

*Disclosure/material fact*

March Cabaret Club and Casino Ltd was the owner of premises in March, Cambridgeshire and carried on the business suggested by the name, that of cabaret restaurant and casino. The club's premises and contents were insured against loss or damage by fire and other perils by a policy issued by London Assurance (part of Sun Alliance and London Group).

A fire occurred in September 1970 and a claim was submitted in respect of both buildings and contents damage for £27,024.

The insurer declined to pay the claim on the grounds of non-disclosure of a material fact. The club, as a limited company, sued for payment.

This case involved other matters, but for the purpose of the text only that one aspect is relevant.

The club originally had insurance cover with another insurer, but in 1967 it sought to increase premiums considerably. The Sun Alliance and London Group was approached, via brokers, and offered the risk. In the course of negotiations Sun Alliance and London Group made it clear that it considered the quality of the management of the club to be an important material fact, and evidence to this effect was made available to the court.

The material fact which the insurers contended should have been disclosed at the renewal of the policy in April 1970 was that a director of the club had been convicted of a criminal offence.

S was a shareholder in the club, and he and his wife were the only directors.

In 1969, after the insurance policy had been in force for some time, S was charged with possession of stolen furs. He pleaded not guilty to the charge, but at his trial which took place after renewal of the policy in April 1970, he was convicted. He did not appeal.

In this civil action against the insurer it would have been possible for him to bring evidence to prove that, in spite of the conviction, he was not guilty of the offence. However, the court was told that he decided not to do so, partly to avoid subjecting his wife and father to the further ordeal of giving evidence.

The judge in this action, Mr Justice May, had therefore to accept the conviction as a fact, and as the offence had taken place before the renewal of the policy in April 1970, he also found that it should have been disclosed then as a material fact.

After considering the legal authorities Mr Justice May held also that the duty to disclose material facts and circumstances arose outside the contract of insurance and is not an implied term of the contract. He also confirmed the view that although a question on a proposal form indicated that the information requested is material, it should not be assumed from the absence of a question that other information is not material.

# Mark Rowlands v Berni Inns Ltd

## *Tenant/fire policy*

Mark Rowlands Ltd was the owner of property at 10/12 Lambs Lane and 6/12 Albion Place, Leeds.

On 27 January 1980, a serious fire occurred at the premises.

The fire damage to the building was subsequently agreed at £1,429,166.

An action was started by the landlord's insurers (Legal and General), under its rights of subrogation against Berni Inns Ltd, the tenant of the part of the building in which the fire had originated.

The grounds of the action were negligence/nuisance on the part of Berni Inns Ltd as it was agreed that the fire was electrical in origin and that this had arisen because of the fault of Berni Inns Ltd.

By way of a counter claim, Berni Inns claimed damages on the grounds that the landlords were in breach of the terms of the lease and they also sought a declaration that the fire insurer was liable to indemnify it (Berni Inns) in respect of the cost of rebuilding and reinstating the premises. In the lease the tenant covenanted:

> to pay to the Landlord a sum of . . . money equal to the amount . . . which the Landlord shall . . . expend in effecting . . . the insurance of the demised premises and being a fair proportion . . . of premiums paid in respect of insuring the Landlord's premises in their full rebuilding value . . . including three years rack rent of the demised premises . . . against loss or damage by fire . . . and such sum . . . shall be paid to the Landlord on demand on the rent day in each year . . .

This provision was referred to as requiring the tenant to pay an "insurance rent".

The tenant also covenanted to maintain the property ". . . damage by . . . insured risks excepted . . ."

The landlord covenanted to keep ". . . the demised premises insured against loss or damage by the insured risks and to lay out any monies received under such insurance in rebuilding and reinstating . . ."

The landlord did in fact take out a policy which insured against, *inter alia*, fire and the insurers agreed to pay "the value of the property".

The persons named in the policy were Mark Rowlands Ltd as mortgagor and the Legal and General as mortgagee; there was no reference to Berni Inns Ltd.

A feature in this case is that there had been correspondence between

Berni Inns' brokers and Mark Rowlands Ltd in the matter of endorsing the name and interest of Berni Inns on the policy. It was suggested that this indicated that the insurance should be for the benefit of the landlord and the tenant.

In the lower court it was concluded that

> ... the true inference to be drawn from the covenants in the lease and from the facts disclosed in the correspondence passing between the defendants and the plaintiffs' insurance brokers ... is that the plaintiffs are to be regarded as having insured the entire premises for the joint benefit of themselves and of the defendants, their tenants ...

The Court of Appeal also considered the question of insurable interest on the part of the tenant, but that is not germaine to the present considerations.

The subrogation action by the insurer against the tenant failed as it was, in effect, seeking to recover from its own insured.

Several cases were cited but *Mumford Hotels v Wheler* (1963) is particularly interesting as this case also deals with the point of the tenant paying the insurance premium and thus having the benefit of the policy.

# North British and Mercantile Insurance Company v London, Liverpool and Globe Insurance Company

## Contribution

This action was instituted

for the purpose of ascertaining the liability of certain fire insurance companies under policies granted by them in respect of the loss by fire of a large amount of grain and seed belonging to Messrs Rodocanachi and Co, Merchants, and stored in the granaries of Messrs Barnett and Co, Wharfingers at Rotherhithe.

Policies effected by Barnett and Co were with several offices and were intended to cover the loss of grain in its granaries or under its care.

One of these policies was with the North British and Mercantile for the period 25 December 1870 to 25 December 1876 and the policy afforded cover in respect of loss or damage by fire to property ". . . the assured's own, in trust, or on commission, for which they are responsible (in no case to exceed the market value of the same immediately anterior to the fire) in the King and Queen Granaries Rotherhithe".

There was also a condition of average which was substantially in the words of the modern condition of average and the policy also contained the following Condition 2.

But it is at the same time declared and agreed that if any property included in such average shall, at the breaking out of any fire, be insured by any other policy in this or any other office whether subject to average or not, which shall apply to part of the buildings of places or the property to which such average extends, then this policy shall not cover the same except only as regards any excess value beyond the amount of such more specific insurance, which said excess is declared to be under the protection of this policy and subject to average as aforesaid.

There were two other conditions which were important in the context of this action, viz:

(9), if at the time of any loss or damage by fire happening to any property hereby insured, there be any other subsisting insurance or insurances, whether affected by the insured or by any other person, covering the same property, this company shall not be liable to pay or contribute more than its rateable proportion of such loss or damage.

(10), in all cases where any other subsisting insurance or insurances, whether effected by the insured or by any other person, covering any other property hereby insured, either exclusively or together with any other property in and subject to the same risk only, shall be subjected to average, the insurance on such property under this policy shall be subjected to average in like manner.

The similarity to the standard fire policy is apparent.

Barnett's other policies contained similar provisions.

Rodocanachi and Co had its own grain stored in the granary of Barnett and Co, and one of its policies was effected with the North British and Mercantile and contained similar conditions to those in Barnett's own policy. One of its other policies did not contain a condition similar to condition ten as previously recited.

On the 14 December 1871 a serious fire occurred at the granary and property to the value of £41,480 owned by Rodocanachi was destroyed. In fact the whole value of the damage sustained was £127,459.

By custom of trade Barnett and Co was responsible to its customers for the safe custody of the goods in its granaries and was liable to make good the loss by fire in whatever way it occurred.

There was much debate between the insurers as to precisely who was responsible for the loss and each contributed to a common fund to settle the claims and this action then followed in order to establish the respective responsibilities.

The North British, acting in its capacity as the grantors of one of the policies issued to Rodocanachi, alleged that it was under no liability on the grounds that Barnett and Co, the wharfinger, must be taken to have indemnified the merchants. North British argued further that if it was obliged to pay Rodocanachi it was entitled to the benefits to all rights of action against Barnett and Co. There was also argument about the question of the conditions incorporating reference to more specific cover.

The London, Liverpool and Globe, as grantor of policies to Barnett and Co, argued that it had no liability under its policies as it only effected a counter indemnity to Barnett and Co to cover its liability to indemnify Rodocanachi and the full value of Rodocanachi and Co's grain was already covered by its own policies. It further argued that under the ninth condition all the companies whose policies were subsisting at the time of the loss were only liable to contribute their rateable proportion of the loss.

During the course of his judgement Jessel M R confirmed the liability of the wharfinger as being in the same position as a common carrier and thus being responsible for the safe custody of the goods entrusted to his care and continued to say that a wharfinger makes a charge to his customer to remunerate him for, amongst other things, the risks attending his trade.

He took the view that Rodocanachi had acted as prudent merchants in insuring the grain and then said

> The question which I have to decide is this, whether, a fire having occurred and a great loss having been sustained the companies who are liable on the merchants' policies are liable to contribute anything to the amount of that loss which the wharfingers' policies alone would be more than sufficient to cover.

He then continued

> . . . what was the true position in law of the companies granting the merchants policies as regard Rodocanachi and as regards Barnett. It appears to me that Barnett and Co, not being parties to the contract of indemnity entered into by Rodocanachi and Co could not derive any benefit from that contract as between themselves and Rodocanachi and Co and if a fire had occurred as it did occur and Rodocanachi and Co sued Barnett and Co the latter must have paid under their admitted liability the whole amount of the loss.

He then suggested the proposition that the alternative course could have been that Rodocanachi and Co could have made a claim under its own policy and said

> It cannot be denied that, if they had taken that course then the insurance companies who had granted the merchants' policies must have paid the amount of the insurance effected by those policies not withstanding Rodocanachi and Co had a remedy against Barnett and Co.

On this basis, of course, there would have been the question of subrogation against Barnett and Co. He indicated that on the basis of the various rights of action here and the absolute responsibility of Barnett and Co there was really no need to deal with the matter further. He did, however, say

> But there was a very important question raised as to the wording of the policies, and whether my opinion be or be not worth anything, I think it right to give it, for the right of persons who may be interested in these matters on further occasions. The policies, I must say, are not well worded.
>
> The word property as used in several conditions means not the actual chattel but the interests of the insured therein. What is the meaning of the words "covering the same property" in the ninth condition? They cannot mean the actual chattel. The most absurd consequences would follow if you read those words in that sense. I am satisfied that this condition was put in to apply to cases where it is the same property that is the subject matter of the insurance and the interests are the same.

He then made some general comments, and said, "I think it my duty to make the instrument rational . . ."
And he concluded

> I am therefore of the opinion that there is no ground for exempting the grantees of the wharfingers' policies from their liability to pay the whole amount.

There was then an appeal and in the judgement Lord Justice James said

> The case is this: Barnett being liable to make good any loss by fire of the goods to Rodocanachi, insured the goods in one office, and Rodocanachi for its own protection insured the goods in another office. There was no communication between the two offices or between the two persons insuring. Under these circumstances it seems to me to be utterly impossible to say that there could have been any contribution. Contribution exists where the thing is done by the same person against the same loss and to prevent a man first of all from recovering more than the whole loss or if he recovers the whole loss from one which he could have recovered from the other, then to make the parties contribute rateably. But that only applies where there is the same person insuring the same interests with more than one office.

Lord Justice Mellish confirmed that he held the same opinion and continued

> Now I do not know of any English cases in the subject of contribution as applied to fire policies; but I can see no reason why the principle in respect of contribution should not be exactly the same in respect of fire policies as they are in respect of marine policies, and I think if the same person in respect of the same right insures in two offices, there is no reason why they should not contribute in equal proportions in respect of a fire policy as they would in the case of a marine policy. The rule is perfectly established in the case of the marine policy that contribution only applies where it is an insurance by the same person having the same rights and does not apply where different persons insure in respect of different rights.

Thus the fundamental rules regarding contribution between policies were established.

# Pawsey v Scottish Union and National

## Proximate cause

Alfred Pawsey and Company insured stock in trade at 104 Harbour Street, Kingston, Jamaica, with the Scottish Union and National which had issued four policies. Each of the first three policies incorporated the following exclusion:

> ... loss or damage by fire occasioned by or happening through ... earthquakes.

The fourth policy incorporated an exclusion whereby the policy did not cover:

> ... Loss or damage by fire during (unless it be proved by the insured that the loss or damage was not occasioned thereby) or in consequence of ... earthquake.

On 14 January 1907, the stock in trade at 104 Harbour Street, owned by Pawsey and Company was destroyed by fire. About 3.30 pm on this day a violent earthquake occurred, the duration of which was about half a minute. During the following night and day minor shocks occurred but the real damage was done by the first shock. Three fires broke out in Kingston about the same time as the earthquake at 3.30 pm.

One of these fires was some distance from the insured's premises at Harbour Street, another fire was in King Street about a quarter of a mile away, but the third fire broke out in 92 Harbour Street "about six numbers to the east of [104 Harbour Street] but separated therefrom ... by the width of [a street crossing Harbour Street]".

The essential point at issue was whether the fire causing the damage at 92 Harbour Street was caused by earthquake and was thus an excluded fire and whether this fire had spread from 92 to 104 or from King Street to Harbour Street.

The Scottish Union and National argued that the fire which destroyed 104 Harbour Street was due to the extension of the fire originating in 92 Harbour Street and that this fire arose independently of any other fire and that it was caused by earthquake.

It was contended further that even if this were not so and it could be argued that the damage was an extension of the King Street fire this fire was also an earthquake fire.

The evidence available to demonstrate the origin of the fire which did spread was confused. There was, of course, much damage caused by the earthquake which it was suggested, for example, had destroyed buildings and thereby prevented the spread of the fire which had originated at 92 Harbour Street.

Pawsey and Company argued that the fire which destroyed its premises had originated in King Street and this fire had been in full blaze 30–45 minutes before the fire was observed at 104 Harbour Street.

The outbreak of fire at 92 Harbour Street was put at an interval of 30–45 minutes after the earthquake at 3.30 pm and the Privy Council considered that it did not follow so quickly after the shock "so as to lead to any very strong presumption that the one event was the cause of the other".

The prime point of the insurer's case was that the fire at 92 Harbour Street had started when boxes of matches in the stores had become ignited because when they fell from the shelves during the earthquake some matches had come into contact with "the prepared surface" and became ignited.

Various questions had been put to the jury at the trial and the appeal to the Privy Council was whether the jury had been reasonable in reaching its conclusions on the evidence.

The questions decided by the trial jury were:

(a)  Was the fire which destroyed the property of Pawsey and Company caused by an earthquake? They concluded it was not.

(b)  Did the fire occur during or in consequence of an earthquake? They concluded it did not.

(c)  Was there any intervening force sufficient of itself to cause the fire to destroy the property of Pawsey and Company? The jury did not answer this question.

The Privy Council concluded that the appeal should be dismissed, the jury having reached a reasonable conclusion.

The classic definition of proximate cause was given in the original trial by Justice Lamb:

> The active efficient cause which sets in motion a chain of events which brings about a result, without the intervention of any force started and working actively from a new or independent source.

# Stoneham v The Ocean, Railway and General Accident Insurance Company

Mr A R Walker had a policy of insurance with the Ocean which was in the nature of a personal accident policy which provided that in the event of the assured sustaining

> any bodily injury caused by any external accident . . . and if the assured shall die, solely from the effects of such accident . . . the Company shall pay . . . the assigns of the assured the sum of £100.

There was a provision in the policy "that this policy shall be subject to the conditions endorsed hereon which shall be considered as incorporated herein".
One of the conditions in the policy said:

> In the event of non fatal injury by an accident occurring to the Assured notice in writing shall be given to the Company . . . within seven days of the occurrence thereof.

Another condition said:

> In case of fatal accident notice thereof must be given to the Company at the head office in London within the like time of seven days.

Mr Walker was accidentally drowned in Jersey and notice was not given to the company in accordance with the last mentioned condition. It was accepted that under the circumstances of the case, such notice could not have been given.
The prime question before the court was whether the condition requiring notice of a fatal accident within seven days of its happening was a condition precedent to the right of the representative of the assured to recover on the policy. The court considered that this was a question of pure construction. Matthew J said

> The policy is expressed to be made subject to certain conditions; the words are, not that these conditions shall be considered as conditions precedent to liability, but, "provided also that this policy shall be subject to the conditions endorsed hereon which shall be considered as incorporated herein".

He continued during the course of his judgement to draw attention to a particular condition of the policy regarding notices of change of occupa-

tion, etc which included the words "In default of . . . so doing, this policy shall become absolutely void . . ."
He concluded by saying that:

The notice is not stated to be a condition of liability, nor is there any stipulation that if no notice is given the policy shall be void. The clause is probably inserted in order to save the Company from the extra expense which they would incur if they had to investigate the circumstances of accidents at long intervals after their occurrence . . . The giving of notice of the accident within seven days is not a condition precedent to the enforcement of the policy.

# Victor Melik and Company Limited v Norwich Union and Kemp

*Warranty, condition precedent to liability*

Victor Melik and Company Limited owned a warehouse which was used to store treated leather skins and which was protected by an alarm.

Norwich Union, the insurer paid a claim of £96,290 following a break in and theft in October 1977. It advised Melik that it required additional protections before agreeing to provide further insurance cover. The work necessary to provide the additional protections was completed on 16 December 1977.

The alarm was connected by a (then) GPO telephone line to a control centre. That control centre would, if it received a message, advise the keyholder and the police.

On the 20th December, Melik and Company was informed that there was fault on the alarm line to the Control Centre. The plaintiff found that the telephones were not working. The alarm was reset to operate the bell only and maintenance contractors and the GPO were advised. The plaintiff also took the trouble to ask the police to increase their patrols near the premises. Upon enquiry the second defendants, Melik's insurance agents, assured the company that the insurance cover was still in operation.

On 21 December, the GPO informed Melik and Company that the fault was "external" and a different team of engineers would have to be sent for. The alarm was still set for bell operation only.

In fact, it transpired, that the thieves had taken off a manhole cover and when inside had cut the telephone wires from the premises. They pushed the cut wires back into a cylinder to hide the fact that they had been cut, replaced the manhole cover and awaited developments. In this way, they were able to trick the engineers who were unable to find the "fault".

On the 22 December 1977 thieves entered the premises and, taking advantage of the absence of the telephone warning, committed a further theft. The amount of the claim was £222,038.90.

The policy had an alarm condition which read:

It is a condition precedent to liability that
   a.  The burglar alarm installed at the premises is kept in efficient working order
   b.  The maintenance contract company is immediately advised of any defect
   c.  The burglar alarm is kept in full operation at all times when the premises are unattended.

The insurer repudiated liability for the claim, arguing that the alarm had not been kept in efficient order and that Victor Melik and Company should have arranged a security guard.

It was held that the burglar alarm was not required to be in efficient working order; it was only required to be "kept" in efficient working order.

It was the view of the court that the use of the word "kept" implied a requirement that before there could be a breach of the condition, the insured must be aware of the facts which give rise to the alarm not being in efficient working order. So far as the court was concerned, the alarm was in efficient working order; it was the Post Office line outside which was not. Therefore, the first defendants were not entitled to avoid liability on the grounds of a breach of the condition.

The judge also considered the situation with regard to the authority of the agent, but that is not relevant to this discussion.

# Weddell and Another v Road Transport and General Insurance Company Limited

*Exclusion clauses*

This was by way of a special case stated by an arbitrator.

On 22 May 1930 J R Weddell arranged an insurance with the Road Transport and General and condition four provided that

> if at any time any claim arises under this policy there is any other existing insurance covering the same loss, damage or liability the company shall not be liable . . . to pay or contribute more than its rateable proportion of any loss, damage, compensation, costs or expense. Provided always that nothing in this condition shall impose on the company any liability from which but for this condition it would have been relieved under the provisions of section II of this policy.

Section II of the policy provided that

> The company will indemnify the insured in the event of injury or damage caused by or through or in connection with any motor car [described in the schedule] . . . against all sums including claimant's costs and expenses which the insured shall become legally liable to pay in respect of . . . accidental . . . injury . . .

There was further provision to "at the request of the insured, treat as though he were insured any relative . . . while driving such motor car . . ."

On 19 August 1929 L W Weddell the brother of J R Weddell had arranged a motor policy with the Cornhill and they agreed to indemnify him against all sums which he should become legally liable to pay by way of compensation "for accidental . . . injury to any person . . ."

The policy continued at section L "The indemnity granted . . . is hereby extended to cover the insured whilst driving any private motor car not belonging to him for pleasure or professional purposes if no indemnity is afforded the insured by any other insurance".

There was a condition in the Cornhill policy that notice of accident or claim should be made within three days.

L W Weddell was driving his brother's car on 4 August 1930 when he accidentally injured Mr F Ward and a claim for damages was made on behalf of Ward against L W Weddell. He failed to tell the Cornhill within the stipulated time of three days and the company repudiated liability on that ground. Ward subsequently began an action against L W Weddell claiming damages and on the 5 November 1930 J R Weddell wrote to the Road Transport and General requesting it to treat his brother L W Weddell "as himself in the matter of the above claim".

The Road Transport and General repudiated liability.

In the course of his judgement Mr Justice Rowlatt said:

> The question is what is the position between the claimant J R Weddell and the respondents the Road Transport Company. L W Weddell cannot recover against the Cornhill Company because he omitted to give them notice of the accident within three days, which by the Cornhill policy is a condition precedent to liability. The arbitrator has held that the Road Transport Company is liable, but by reason of condition four liable only for a rateable proportion, treating the Cornhill policy as being an "other existing insurance" within condition four.

He continued

> It is to be borne in mind that the risk covered by the clause as to a relative or friend is an extension of the scope of the policy. It gives protection to a person other than the assured. So, too, the clause in the Cornhill company's policy covering the assured when driving a car not belonging to him is an extension of the primary purpose of the policy, which is to cover risks to and in connection with a particular car or cars of the assured mentioned in the schedule . . . In my judgement it is unreasonable to suppose that it was intended that clauses such as these should cancel each other (by neglecting in each case the proviso in the other policy) with the result that, on the ground in each case that the loss is covered elsewhere it is covered nowhere. On the contrary . . .

Following elaboration of points he continued

> If one proceeds to apply the same argument to the other policy and lets that re-act upon the policy under construction, one would reach the result that whichever policy one looks at it is always the other one which is effective.
>
> In these circumstances I come to the conclusion that the Cornhill Company (apart from the omission to give the notice) were liable notwithstanding that their policy contained no rateable proportion clause, and I confirm the decision of the Arbitrator.

# Williams v Baltic Insurance Association of London Ltd

*Insurable interest*

On 19 July 1921, Mr E B Williams arranged an insurance in respect of his motor car with the Baltic, the cover being in respect of an indemnity "against all sums for which [he] or any licensed personal friend or relative ... whilst driving the car ... shall become legally liable in compensation ..."

Miss B Williams, the sister of E B Williams, was driving the car on the 27 October 1921 when an accident occurred which resulted in personal injuries to passengers in the car.

In a subsequent action against both Mr and Miss Williams judgement was entered in favour of Mr Williams with costs and for the plaintiffs against Miss Williams for £3162.12s. 3d. including costs. Mr Williams then submitted a claim against the Baltic to indemnify Miss Williams for that sum. During the course of his summing up and judgement Roche J made reference to the points made in the pleadings regarding the Life Assurance Act 1774 and said

> For a general discussion of the attitude of the law to insurance with or without interest I will simply refer to the very excellent and useful work of Mr Macgillivray on Insurance Law. It is sufficient to say that there is nothing in the common law of England which prohibits insurance even if no interest exists. It may be necessary to show interest, but there is no general prohibition in law. It is said, however, that the Act of 1774 prevents an insurance such as this [reference in pleadings was made to the Life Assurance Act 1774, sections 1, 2, 3 and 4]. It is said that Mr Bransby Williams has no interest in Miss Williams' liability and therefore cannot recover; that Miss Bransby Williams who might be said to be interested, cannot recover, because her name is not inserted in the policy; and that at all events section 3 of the Act prevents Mr Bransby Williams recovering anything beyond his own interest.

Reference was made to *Waters v Monarch* which was a cover arranged by a warehouseman for goods in trust in which the warehouseman had been able to recover as trustee for the customers in respect of their goods. In referring to that case Mr Justice Ross said

> The Court there held that the policy was a policy on goods, and I am satisfied that in this case also the policy is on goods. The motor car is the subject matter of the insurance and a motor car is a chattel or goods ..."

Towards the end of his judgement Mr Justice Ross continued

The general argument that Mr Bransby Williams cannot recover for Miss Bransby Williams because the latter cannot recover for herself, is based upon this, that the insured is Mr Bransby Williams. That I think is begging the question. Mr Bransby Williams is the insured in the sense that he is the person who effected the insurance but it is an insurance for himself and the other persons mentioned in clause 2, and, accordingly the company's contract is to indemnify all such persons in the event of those things happening against which the insurance is effected.

Consideration was then given to the proposition that an insurable interest must subsist at the time a policy is taken out and Mr Justice Ross continued, to suggest that there was no support for the view that an interest must subsist at the time a policy is taken out.

He pointed out that this was decided to the contrary in 1810 in the case *Rhind v Wilkinson*.

He concluded that the decision of the learned arbitrators stating that the Baltic was required to indemnify Miss Williams for the liability which she had sustained was in order.

# APPENDIX I

# Table of cases

# Index

Introduction to theft, all risks and money policies